THE SPIRIT OF '76

From now until 1983, we Americans will celebrate the bicentennial of the greatest event of
our history—the American Revolution. How
we choose to commemorate the founding of our
nation will shape the lives of generations yet to
come. Will we be content with fireworks and
plastic liberty bells? Or will we use the anniversary of the Revolution as a time to rededicate
ourselves and our country to the sacred ideals
our ancestors fought for two hundred years ago?

VOICES OF
THE AMERICAN REVOLUTION

by

The Peoples Bicentennial Commission

A Nationwide Citizen Organization Dedicated
to Restoring the Democratic Principles That
Shaped the Birth of This Republic

The Peoples Bicentennial Commission staff for
VOICES OF THE AMERICAN REVOLUTION

Major writer:
Ted Howard

Contributors:
Page Smith
Charlie Jones
Noreen Banks

Editorial Assistants:
Kathy Johnson
Bob Leonard
Jeremy Rifkin
Sheila Rollins
Bill Peltz

Voices
of
The American Revolution

THE
PEOPLES
BICENTENNIAL COMMISSION

RLI:
VLM 11 (VLR 10-12)

IL 8-adult

VOICES OF THE AMERICAN REVOLUTION
A Bantam Book published January 1975

All rights reserved.
Copyright © 1974 by Peoples Bicentennial Commission

This book may not be reproduced in whole or in part, by mimeograph or any other means, without permission. For information address: Bantam Books, Inc.

Published simultaneously in the United States and Canada

Bantam Books are published by Bantam Books, Inc. Its trademark, consisting of the words "Bantam Books" and the portrayal of a bantam, is registered in the United States Patent Office and in other countries. Marca Registrada. Bantam Books, Inc., 666 Fifth Avenue, New York, New York 10019.

PRINTED IN THE UNITED STATES OF AMERICA

CONTENTS

The American Revolution Then And Now

INTRODUCTION

On July 4, 1776, when the Continental Congress approved the Declaration of Independence, the western world's first successful revolution against political and economic tyranny was launched. Several years ago, the Associated Press released this news item:

MIAMI (July 4)—Only one person out of 50 approached on Miami streets by a reporter agreed to sign a typed copy of the Declaration of Independence. Two called it "Commie junk," one threatened to call the police, and another warned: "Be careful who you show that kind of antigovernment stuff to, buddy." Comments from those who took the trouble to read the first three paragraphs:

"This is the work of a raver."

"Somebody ought to tell the FBI about this sort of rubbish."

"Meaningless."

"The boss'll have to read this before I can let you put it in the shop window. But politically, I can tell you he don't lean that way. He's a Republican."

3

In the last few years, we Americans have experienced domestic and foreign crises as great as any that faced our Nation at its birth two hundred years ago. The list is long and familiar: the war in Indochina, civil-rights agitation, assassinations of political leaders, massive inflation and unemployment, economic chaos over food and energy, the tortuous battle over the impeachment of a President, and on and on. But as that reporter in Miami discovered, an even greater crisis has hit our country: the uncertainty we all feel about what America stands for today. While other national problems gain public attention in our newspaper headlines and on the evening news, this crisis gets little notice. Yet this confusion over our basic values as a people lies at the root of all of our other national ills.

It all boils down to a single, basic question: What does it mean today to be a patriotic American? Two hundred years ago, people had a ready answer: a patriotic American was anyone who firmly believed in the democratic principles of the Declaration of Independence and our American Revolution—plain and simple. But today, when only one out of fifty Americans will endorse our Nation's founding document, something is drastically wrong. Crises in foreign policy, in the economy, in political leadership will come and go, but a people who have lost sight of their roots and ideals will soon fall prey to those very same "dark, designing knaves" our ancestors fought a revolution against.

The problem is as old as our country. Tom Paine, the chief propagandist of the American Revolution and the author of *Common Sense*, wrote a prescription for his fellow Americans that is still valid:

It is at all times necessary, and more particularly so during the progress of a revolution, and until right ideas confirm themselves by habit, that we frequently refresh our patriotism by reference to first principles. It is by tracing things to their origin that we learn to understand them, and it is by keeping that line and that origin always in view that we never forget them.

To our ancestors, this was not a vague notion. It was "reference to first principles" that sustained the Revolution. In revolutionary times every institution, leader, law and political viewpoint was deemed a just target for public scrutiny. The test was a simple one: "What role does this leader (or law or philosophy) play in building and preserving our democratic birthrights?" As King George III learned, even a tradition as ancient as the monarchy could be challenged when an institution was judged directly by the people and found wanting. "Tracing things to their origins" taught our ancestors a basic truth: people make institutions; people can change them.

It is this continuing reference—the endless questioning, examining, arguing, debating and even standing up and fighting when necessary—that is the real substance of the American Revolution. True, the typical historical accounts of the "Spirit of '76" focus on a handful of famous men, a series of battles and dates, and the usual empty platitudes about the "War for Independence." If this were all the American Revolution was really about, it wouldn't have more than passing interest to us today.

The American Revolution was earth-shaking two hundred years ago, and has profound meaning for us today, because it showed that ordinary people who believed and lived the principles of democracy could take on the greatest empire and the most powerful monarch in the world, and win.

It is ordinary people, who live and die in

John Hancock

Sam¹ Adams · Phil. Livingston

Rob¹ Treat Paine   W⁰ Floyd

John Adams   Fran.ˢ Lewis

Elbridge Gerry

Josiah Bartlett   Rich⁴ Stockton

Samª Huntington

Steph. Hopkins   John Hart

Abra Clark   Lewis Morris

John Morton

Matthew Thornton

Roger Sherman   John Penn

Wm Whipple   Jn⁰ Witherspoon

William Ellery   Wm Hooper

Oliver Wolcott   Rob¹ Morris

Benj Franklin   Wm Williams

Wm Paca

Fra.ˢ Hopkinson   Thos Stone

Charles Carroll of Carrollton

Signatures on the Declaration of Independence

obscurity, whose names do not appear on monuments or in the pages of our history books, who are the real force behind all of history. Generals, politicians, poets, saints and tycoons may get the speaking parts, but without "the people" there would be no history. In history, there is no audience: all of us are actors, willing or not. There are 'stars'—the people historians single out to be remembered; and there is a "cast"—literally a 'cast of millions,' without whom the stars could not exist. In a truly democratic society, the stars can rise only to the degree that they express the hopes and dreams of the rest of the cast.

At certain moments the cast emerges from the relative obscurity of its daily existence to assert its power. The American Revolution was such a moment, and the 'stars' of the time knew it. When Thomas Jefferson was asked where he gained the inspiration to write the Declaration of Independence, he replied that he had but to look into the hearts of the people, where he found its revolutionary principles indelibly stamped. What Jefferson and the other founding radicals learned, and what we would do well to remember, was the fundamental truth that "Power resides always in the body of the people." Once they knew this, the people had only to use it, and that was just what they did: two million colonial Americans, living in a remote wilderness far from the center stage of history, asserted themselves with startling boldness and resolution. As a result of their act, the course of world history was changed.

It is the Declaration of Independence, that gives us the best sense of what that Revolution of two hundred years ago meant to the people who lived it. The Declaration articulated all the dreams, ideas, principles, hopes and yearnings engendered by the revolutionary movement that began with the agitation against the Stamp Act of 1765. But it was in the plain fact that women and men were willing to die for the principles which it set forth that the Declaration derived its ultimate power. Had it been otherwise, the Declaration of Independence would have been merely an historical curiosity: interesting to scholars, but of little practical consequence.

Two centuries ago, Americans committed their "lives, fortunes, and sacred honors" to the ideals of this Declaration. Today we scarcely know anything about our founding document and the people who lived it. It's time for us to refresh our *own* patriotism, and find out what it once meant to be an American. It's time once again for "We, the people," to assert that ultimate power which lies within us. What better way to celebrate the two hundredth anniversary of the first American Revolution?

To understand our founding democratic principles, and what they can mean to us today, we must trace our country back to its origins; back to the events which set the stage for our Declaration of Independence, and the American Revolutionary philosophy it represented.

A REVOLUTION IN THE MAKING

When the 1760s began in America, none of the two million people who inhabited the thirteen colonies had any reason to believe earth-shaking changes would take place in their lifetime. Since the arrival of the first Europeans over 150 years before, America had been a place far removed from the center stage of history.

What few people on either side of the Atlantic realized was just how different Americans had become from their relatives in Europe in that short time. Three thousand miles away from the kings and feudal systems of the "old world," the colonists had changed dramatically. If Americans could not themselves understand the transformation that had been taking place during that century and a half, recently arrived immigrants could. A Frenchman, Hector St. John de Crevecoeur, recorded his excited observations of this "new world" mentality:

> In this great American asylum, the poor of Europe have by some means met together. Urged by a variety of motives, here they came. Every thing has tended to regenerate them; new laws, a new mode of living, a new social system; here they are become men: in Europe

they were so many useless plants, wanting
vegetative mould and refreshing showers . . .
but now by the power of transplantation . . .
they have taken root and flourished . . . What
then is the American, this new man? Here
individuals of all races are melted into a new
race of men, whose labors and posterity will
one day cause great changes in the world . . .
The American is a new man, who acts upon
new principles; he must therefore entertain
new ideas, and form new opinions. From in-
voluntary idleness, servile dependence, penury and useless labor, he has passed to toils
of a very different sort . . . This is an American.

It was this 'new American' that was to come
into conflict with the ruling authority of the
Crown in the 1760s. It all began when the Government of King George III, having decided that the
New World had for too long been left to its own
devices, attempted to draw the colonies closer to
"the parent state." By doing so, the Royal Government unwittingly showed Americans that their
destiny could lie within themselves, and not with
kings and empires.

The King's first attempt to increase his control
over his American subjects began in 1765. Seeking funds to pay the debts incurred by the French
and Indian War, George Grenville, First Minister
in the Tory government, decided to impose a tax
in the form of stamps on legal documents, newspapers, and—as Americans saw it—on practi-
cally everything else in sight. During the debate
over the tax in Parliament, Colonel Isaac Barre,
an Englishman and an ardent supporter and
friend of the American cause, declared that such
a tax would be viewed as unconstitutional in the
colonies. He described earlier acts of the Government and its officials in America that had "made

King George

Queen Charlotte

the blood of those sons of liberty boil within
them," and warned of dire consequences if the
tax were passed.

A substantial majority of the members of the
House of Commons ignored Barre's warning. The
Stamp Act was passed and the American Revolution, in a sense, started at once: the ordinary
people of the country refused to allow the stamps
to be used. It was over ten years before the final
break occurred, but never again would Americans
give wholehearted allegiance to the King's Government.

The Stamp Act is probably best remembered
for the riots associated with it. Throughout
America "men of quality" were astounded by the
popular fury and the extent to which the newly
self-discovered rebels would go to prevent the use
of the stamps. In one typical demonstration, on
August 14, 1765, the Sons of Liberty of Boston,
formed specifically to stand against the Act,
christened the first Liberty Tree by hanging an
effigy of the Governor's brother-in-law. The turmoil in Boston continued until November 1, when
the Act was to go into effect. Another effigy was
strung up, this time of the Prime Minister, as

Anti-Stamp Act Cartoon

crowds marched in solemn procession to the tolling of bells. Later in the day, the effigy was found hanging from the town gallows. Finally, on December 17, the Governor's brother-in-law, Andrew Oliver, was forced to stand beneath the Tree and publicly resign his commission as a stamp distributor before two thousand irate citizens.

Other actions followed throughout the colonies: more forced resignations of stamp agents; destruction of Government officials' homes by angry mobs; the burning of crates of unused stamps. In the end, the opposition was so widespread that there is but a single recorded instance of the stamps ever being used. The unthinkable had happened: the people rebelled, on their own and with little leadership, and fought the mightiest empire in the world at the time to a standstill. When the Government did the only thing it could—repeal the Act—Americans felt as though they had slain a giant.

Celebrations took place from Massachusetts to Georgia. John Adams' description of the mood in Boston serves as a testimony to the spirit of the Stamp Act rebels:

JOHN BULL.

Such a day has not been seen in Boston before or since. The Bells of Dr. Blye's church began the tune at one in the morning. The chime in Christ Church made response. The steeples were hung with flags. Liberty Tree was adorned all day with banners and illuminated in the evening, till the boughs could hold no more. Music was heard in the streets before daybreak. Subscriptions were raised to release those who were in jail for debt, from confinement. The country people came in thousands. The whole town was splendidly illuminated. The Common was covered with multitudes. Rockets blazed in every quarter. And to crown all, a magnificent pyramid was erected which shone with the blaze of 300 lamps.

The Stamp Act movement should have taught the King and his ministers of the power within this "new American." Crevecoeur had noted it during a period of tranquility; but after 1765 it was aroused. The protests of the 1760s said to all: "This new American is unstoppable." Here was a person no longer willing to be dependent

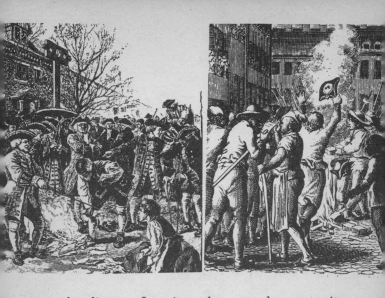

or subordinate. Leaving the complex constitutional arguments up to the handful of intellectuals, lawyers and pamphleteers, the American simply knew that he or she was unwilling to accept domination by those who knew or cared little or nothing for the interests, ambitions, and needs of his new-world mentality.

This general attitude *should* have been apparent to the King and his Government, but it was not. After the repeal of the Stamp Act, most Americans appeared to view the Government's attempt at taxation without representation as an exceptional instance of high-handed callousness. *Now*, the great majority of the colonists hoped, the Government would listen to reason. But others—a handful at first, but a constantly growing number—saw the possibility as remote. "You might as well hope to bind up a hungry tiger with a cobweb," wrote Abigail Adams, "as to hold such debauched patriots in the visionary chains of decency, or to charm them with the intellectual beauty of truth and reason."

Hardly had the dust stirred by the Stamp Act

Patrick Henry

settled, than the British ministers, still looking for money to run the Government, decided to place a tax (the Townshend Duties) on certain items imported into the colonies, especially glass, paint, and tea.

Complex legalistic arguments were offered by the King's cronies to make it appear as if this tax were somehow different, and so more justified, than the Stamp Act. But it all amounted to the same thing, and once again the protests began. This time however, moderates who had

protests the Stamp Act

watched in horror the "excesses" of the mobs of common people during the agitation of the mid-'60s, moved to curb new turmoil by assuming positions of leadership in the new anti-tax movement. These men sought to avoid the popular outbursts of the Stamp Act riots, and were more concerned with riding herd on their more radical countrymen and women than with dealing a blow to governmental tyranny. Because of this moderate stance, the new protests achieved only partial success: the repeal of some duties, but not

all. These results caused a great deal of bitterness and distrust between the majority of common Americans and their moderate leaders.

When the anti-tax movement finally died down, Americans found that it had left behind several new institutions that were to take a hand in shaping events of the Seventies. The first was of the colonists' own making: the "associations". To carry out economic boycotts against those British goods taxed by the Townshend Duties, "non-importation associations" were established in cities and towns throughout America. These associations, along with the older Sons of Liberty and the soon-to-be formed "committees of correspondence," became the network that the colonial radicals used to mobilize their fellow citizens in opposition to the Government. The Government's new institution, a standing army made up of the King's Redcoats (soldiers sent from England to enforce the King's laws and called Redcoats because of their bright red uniforms), chilled the hearts of all freedom-loving Americans. King George, angered over the contempt shown royal authority during the Stamp Act riots, and anticipating renewed turmoil over the Townshend Duties, began stationing his troops in Boston and other cities.

Sent to America to maintain law and order, the British soldiers provoked mob violence, and then fired upon unarmed Americans to suppress it. Bostonians, unrivaled in the jealous defense of their liberties, were convinced that the stationing of troops in their city would soon lead to its formal occupation by the British. Then, on the cold evening of March 5, 1770, an unruly crowd of men and boys—once again, those ordinary people who make history—confronted a garrison of armed Redcoats. Insults were exchanged, snowballs and sticks were thrown, and finally the inevitable shots were fired. When the smoke cleared, four patriots lay dead; another would die soon after from his wounds. There were more

On the Death of Five
young Men who
was Murthered,
March 5th 1770.
By the 29th Regi-
ment.

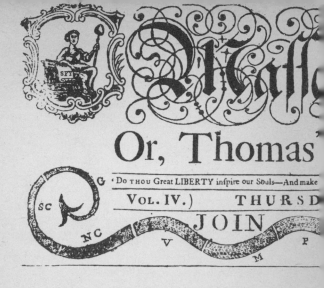

Or, Thomas'

'Do thou Great LIBERTY inspire our Souls—And make

VOL. IV.)   THURSD

JOIN

protests, especially in Massachusetts, but they were minor compared to those of earlier days. Burning stamped paper and hanging effigies was one thing, but facing off against armed troops was another, and many Americans decided to step back for a while, and ask themselves if they believed in their cause enough to give their lives for it. It was the ultimate question that those who demand revolutionary change have had to face from the very beginning of human society. After this day it would take a few years for Americans to come to an answer.

Those years following the Boston Massacre have been called "The Quiet Years" by historians, and they must have appeared so when viewed from the throne room 3,000 miles away. They might have been quiet, but they were not idly spent. It might be said that during these years Americans went to school in the principles of democracy. A theory of government and human rights, a theory that became increasingly more revolutionary as it was developed and debated,

THE
chusetts Spy
Boston Journal.

Lives in THY Poſſeſſion happy—Or, our Deaths glorious in THY juſt Defence.'

Y, JULY 7, 1774.   (NUMB. 179.

OR   DIE

NJ

NY

NE

became the national dialogue. In their churches, in the college debating societies, in the taverns and pubs of even the smallest towns, Americans were coming to grips with the question that had been demanding an answer from the start: "Which will it be, the Old World or the New?"

While the people in general hammered out their new theory of society, the most committed patriots began to put together the nuts and bolts of an inter-colonial revolutionary network that could be activated at a moment's notice. "Divide and conquer" had been the age-old motto of tyrants everywhere; it only made sense that America's rebels took "Join or Die" as theirs. Lacking mass communications, patriots formed the Committees of Correspondence, a network of trusted horsemen who were willing to deliver messages between radicals in all parts of the country. The Committees of Correspondence, along with the Sons of Liberty and the Associations, fought to break down the feelings of isolation and hopelessness that the many scattered groups of ardent patriots felt. In a country of thirteen separate colonies, some of them weeks apart on horseback or by ship, the job of this revolutionary network was crucial: to show *all* Americans that they had more in common with each other than any of them alone would ever have with England and the King. In this struggle, Patrick Henry was soon to shout to the Virginia Legislature, "The distinctions between Virginians, Pennsylvanians, New Yorkers, and New Englanders are no more. I am not a Virginian, but an American!"

It was during these quiet years of the early 1770s that Americans moved from resistance to revolution. The "quiet", as it turned out, was just the calm before the storm. Soon, the revolutionary dialogue and organizing of the '70s came into use.

JOIN, or DIE.

THE REVOLUTION BEGINS

The year 1773 began much like any other, but by the time it was over America was never to be the same again. For it was in 1773 that King George—together with his supporters in Parliament and the wealthy business interests who bought the Members' votes for the right price—put out enough rope (or in this case, exceeded their rightful authority sufficiently) to "hang" the British future in America. When the year began, American patriots were debating tyranny in the abstract; by the year's end, the Royal Government had handed them two issues that turned the far-off storm into a full-blown hurricane.

First came "the letters." In late 1772, Benjamin Franklin, then an American representative to the court of King George, managed to obtain confidential Government papers exchanged between Thomas Hutchinson and Andrew Oliver, two of the King's appointed officials in Massachusetts, and Thomas Whately, a member of the King's Ministry in London. The documents, passed from Franklin to Sam Adams to John Hancock, contained passages advocating an abridgement "of what are called English liberties" in America, so that the Royal Government could more closely

25

Benjamin Franklin

control the political affairs of the colonies. The papers, widely reprinted in patriot newspapers and broadsides, stunned and outraged all who read them. Many began listening more closely to the very patriots who had been most severely denounced in the Hutchinson/Oliver documents.

Just as news of the infamous letters was spreading throughout the country, Americans received another bombshell. Lord North, recently appointed head of the Tory Ministry—feeling supremely confident that he had finally managed to cool colonial agitation, and with it, the patriots'

Francis Hutchinson, Royal Governor of Mass.
Frederick, Lord North (Library of Congress)

"misplaced zeal for their fancied rights"—hit upon yet another scheme of taxation.

As they sat down in Parliament to approve the plan, Government officials must have thought that they had finally found the perfect tax package. All the ingredients for success were there. The East India Company, an octopus-like corporation with investments, holdings and private armies around the world, which had lately hit upon hard times, would be bailed out of its financial difficulties with a huge Government subsidy as well as a monopoly on the tea trade to America. Members of Parliament, many of whom were large investors in the EIC, would receive substantial financial benefit. Most importantly, by getting one foot in the door with the tea tax, the Royal Government would set a precedent that would permit taxation that could be increased in later years.

It all seemed so perfect, and the capstone of the Tea Tax looked impossible to beat. By granting the EIC both a subsidy and a monopoly over the tea trade, the price of tea to American consumers would actually drop *below* the price of tea smuggled in from other countries. Lord North and the King assumed that Americans would not oppose a tax that actually lowered the price of goods even if it were imposed without representation. The King, his ministers and the English business community did not know that in the New World people could be willing to sacrifice some of their hard-earned money to preserve a principle of democracy. The battle over the Tea Tax was not for pennies, but for power: who would rule America, the unelected government of the East India Company and Parliament, or the American people?

The Tea Act was approved by the King in April of 1773. For six months colonial radicals lay in wait, developing a proper strategy of response, explaining the issues to their fellow citizens and building support for the time when they would strike. "Put your enemy in the wrong," Sam Adams thundered, "and keep him there!"

The first shipments of taxed tea arrived in colonial ports in the early winter of 1773. From Georgia to New Hampshire, Americans expressed their determination that it should not be landed. In the absence of specific instructions most of the colonial governors allowed the ships carrying the tea to be turned back by crowds of angry patriots, preferring to risk the anger of the King of England rather than the wrath of colonial mobs. But in Massachusetts, Governor Hutchinson, who had had his house destroyed during the Stamp Act riots and who had authored some of the most alarming of the letters leaked by Franklin and Adams, ordered the tea landed.

As the 17th of December neared, the date the tea was to be unloaded in Massachusetts, the attention of the entire colony turned to Griffin's Wharf, where the three tea ships lay moored. Letting the conflict build until the last possible moment, Sam Adams convened an open town meeting on the 16th. Eight thousand Bostonians (out of an entire population of just thirty thousand) turned out for the meeting at Old South Church. After the crowd assembled, a messenger was dispatched to the Governor's palace, demanding one last time that the tea be sent back to England. When word came back of the Governor's refusal, Sam Adams took the stage, shouting, "There is nothing more this meeting can do to save the country." With that, the eight thousand patriots, led by 150 Sons of Liberty dressed as "Mohawks," swarmed down to the docks. That night, as Tories and government officials looked hopelessly on, 342 chests of tea were dumped into the harbor.

The Boston Tea Party was a master-stroke of protest. What had been at the time of the Stamp Act, eight years earlier, an impassioned and spontaneous response to an act seen as arbitrary and unconstitutional, was now as carefully planned and rehearsed as a military operation. Patriots organized into squads knew only the name of their immediate leader. Immediately following the destruction of the tea, substantial rewards were offered by the Crown for the identities of the participants, but not a single person came forward to collect the money. To this day, most of the names of the rebels are unknown.

John Adams saw the event as a model of action for patriots everywhere:

> The people should never rise without doing something to be remembered—something notable and striking. This destruction of the tea is so bold, so daring, so firm, intrepid and inflexible, and it must have so important consequences, and so lasting, that I can't but consider it an epoch in history.

It was all pure, 18th Century guerrilla theater, but it was also deadly serious, this business of

flaunting royal authority and openly destroying corporate property. Sam Adams, realizing the consequences of the action, quickly activated the Committees of Correspondence, sending riders throughout the country to inform other patriots of the Boston Tea Party, and to ask for signs of support. They were quick in coming.

In New York, Philadelphia, Annapolis, and other cities, patriots staged their own tea parties—burning crates of already landed tea, dumping tea chests into harbors and once, even forcing

In 1767 Franklin designed and sent this cartoon to friends. It prophesies the sad plight of Britannia stripped of her colonies.

a ship owner to burn his own vessel. Everywhere, support resolutions passed in town meetings condemned the East India Company and the Tea Tax, and expressed thanks to the patriots of Boston.

The British government reacted to these outrages against property and good order by closing the port of Boston and placing the city under an 18th Century version of a state of siege. Once again, the previous three years of organizing and

The Bostonians in distress (British cartoon after the Tea Party)

propagandizing paid off as other colonies sent supplies of food and money to the beleaguered city. On the day the port of Boston was officially closed, the entire country observed a day of fasting and mourning in support of their fellow patriots. A letter from the Boston Committee of Correspondence expressed what was once the hope of a few radicals, but had now become the majority sentiment: "*All* should be united in this opposition to the liberties of *all*."

Boston cannonaded

Boston Port Bill

Paul Revere's engraving of Tea Party aftermath c. 1775

Finally, in an effort to form a united strategy against these acts of tyranny, a meeting of representatives from twelve of the thirteen colonies was assembled in Philadelphia in September, 1774. The men who came to that first Continental Congress were mostly moderates, far behind the desires of the people, as most of the colonial leaders had been since the days of the Stamp Act. In the midst of growing agitation, they sat and debated, unwilling to make a bold move. After drafting renewed petitions asking the King to recognize the rights of Americans, and advocating a renewed economic boycott, the Congress adjourned, setting May of 1775 as the date for the Second Continental Congress. But even as the

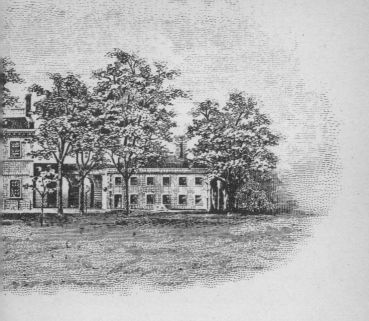

gentlemanly proceedings took place in Philadelphia, the revolution was proceeding throughout the rest of the country.

Armed conflicts between Minutemen (American citizen-soldiers who could be ready to do battle at a minute's notice), and the Redcoats began to break out. The pitched confrontations at Lexington and Concord on April 19, 1775, were but the most memorable of these early battles of the undeclared war. And while some Americans fought—and some died—most Americans were engaged in another monumental struggle, one that had to be resolved before any successful campaign against the King's troops could be waged. It was an emotional, internal battle, one

Members of the Continental Congress leaving Independence Hall

waged within the minds of all Americans. Its object was to cast off the deeply ingrained notion that—regardless of what reason and experience might dictate—somehow kings and all they represented were of profound and vital necessity to happiness and prosperity.

The revolutionary mentality that had been forming since the days of the Stamp Act was still overlaid by thousands of treasured memories of Great Britain and her monarchs. This was the real power the King was counting on to keep his American subjects in line. If George III could have maintained the myth of legitimacy that surrounded him, he never would have had to use his powerful army and navy. Even as the Minutemen fired on the royal troops at Lexington and Concord, they proclaimed their loyalty to the King. The institution of the monarchy had become so deified and entrenched after hundreds of years in power that most Americans simply could not imagine how life would proceed with-

A MINUTE MAN PREPARING FOR WAR.

Tom Paine

out its guiding force. After all, every country Americans knew of at the time was ruled by one crowned head or another.

Into this emotional turmoil stepped Thomas Paine, a recent emigrant from England. Paine, a former corset-maker in London who had been fired for trying to get better working conditions for himself and his fellows, arrived in Philadelphia with a letter from Ben Franklin commending him to the Pennsylvania patriots. After taking stock of the situation in America, Paine quietly began preparing a pamphlet that would forever destroy the arguments that America had any other recourse than revolution. The result was *Common Sense*. Published anonymously, it swept the country.

Common Sense was written by a common man for the common people. It came out of the bitter years of Paine's own life as a laborer in England. Living among his fellow workers, he experienced at first hand the day-to-day abuses of the monarchy. The rights of Americans were being destroyed by this same system, but they at least had the benefit of three thousand miles of ocean between them and the heart of the Empire. No American could ever have written as passionate a statement as did the relatively uneducated and uncultured "Tom" Paine.

Common Sense pulled no punches in its assault on the monarchy; anything short of "separation and independence" it read, would be "mere patchwork." Aiming to destroy the legitimacy of the institution of the monarchy, and sweeping away with it the arguments of the moderates who continued to insist that the *system* was sound and that it was just a few of the *men* who ran it who had stepped out of line, Paine listed, then refuted, every argument in favor of kings. The monarch was descended from God?, Paine asked. He

COMMON SENSE;

ADDRESSED TO THE

INHABITANTS

OF

AMERICA,

On the following interesting

SUBJECTS.

I. Of the Origin and Design of Government in general,
with concise Remarks on the English Constitution.

II. Of Monarchy and Hereditary Succession.

III. Thoughts on the present State of American Affairs.

IV. Of the present Ability of America, with some mis-
cellaneous Reflections.

Man knows no Master save creating HEAVEN,
Or those whom choice and common good ordain.

THOMSON.

PHILADELPHIA;

Printed, and Sold, by R. BELL, in Third-Street.

MDCCLXXVI.

answered himself: "A French bastard (William the Conqueror) landing with an armed banditti and establishing himself King of England against the consent of the natives, is in plain terms a very paltry rascally original. It certainly hath no divinity in it."

The King is kept in check by Parliament? "How came the King by a power which the people are afraid to trust, and always obliged to check? Such a power could not be the gift of a wise people, neither can any power, which needs checking, be from God."

America has received great benefit from its union with the King? "Nothing can be more fallacious than this kind of argument:—we may as well assert that because a child has thrived upon milk, that it is never to have meat, or that the first twenty years of our lives is to become a precedent for the next twenty."

Hereditary succession is the right of kings? "All men being originally equals, no one by birth could have a right to set up his own family in perpetual preference to all others for ever."

The King is our father; Britain is our parent state? "Then the more shame upon her conduct. Even brutes do not devour their young, nor savages make war upon their families."

On and on went the indictment as Paine stripped the myths of legitimacy from the monarchy. By the time he was done, the emperor truly had no clothes. By stripping the monarchy of its supporting myths, Paine showed all who read *Common Sense* that beneath the purple robes and gold crowns, kings are simply the creations of the people. And anything created by people—be it a hay wagon or a pompous prince—can be changed by the people.

Having cleared the ground, Paine went on to speak in no less striking language of the earth-shattering nature of the conflict:

The sun never shined on a cause of greater worth. 'Tis not the affair of a city, a country, a province, or a kingdom, but of a continent— of at least one-eighth part of the habitable globe. 'Tis not the concern of a day, a year, or an age; posterity are virtually involved in the contest, and will be more or less affected even to the end of time by the proceedings now. Now is the seedtime of continental union, faith and honor . . . By referring the matter from argument to arms, a new era for politics is struck—a new method of thinking has arisen. All plans, proposals, etc. prior to the nineteenth of April, i.e. to the commencement of hostilities, are like the almanacs of the last year; which though proper then, are superseded and useless now . . . Everything that is right or reasonable pleads for separation. The blood of the slain, the weeping voice of nature cries, "Tis time to part." Even the distance at which the Almighty hath placed England and America is a strong and natural proof that the authority of the one over the other was never the design of heaven . . . It is repugnant to reason, to the universal order of things, to all examples from former ages, to suppose that this continent can long remain subject to any external power . . . The utmost stretch of human wisdom cannot, at this time, compass a plan, short of separation, which can promise the continent even a year's security. Reconciliation is *now* a fallacious dream. Nature has deserted the connection, and art cannot supply her place.

Common Sense was an openly impassioned piece of propaganda, designed to speak to Americans who had never really cared for fine, legalistic arguments. It reflected the new American mentality developed over the decade since the Stamp Act. No scholar, no graduate of Harvard or Yale, however radical his politics, could have composed such a tract. His class, his background, his education had made him too *conventional* in his language, too academic, too logical, to speak with such power or touch such common chords. To say it was the most successful political pamphlet in history is to do it insufficient credit. *Common Sense* belongs in a category all its own. Published in Philadelphia on January 10, 1776, it was republished everywhere: all through the colonies from Charlestown, South Carolina, to Salem, Massachusetts. It crossed the ocean and was translated into German, French and Dutch. It was even published in London with most of the treasonable strictures against the Crown omitted. There is even a story that, one night, the Queen herself caught her son, the Prince of Wales, reading Paine's work under his covers.

Paine himself estimated that within three months it had sold over a hundred and twenty thousand copies, and many copies were passed from hand to hand until they were stained and ragged. It is probably conservative to estimate that a million Americans read it, or almost half the population of the colonies. *Common Sense* proved the power of words; it showed that a statement of common feelings and emotions coming from the common experiences and dreams of a people can change the course of history.

Patriots everywhere greeted the pamphlet with fervor: "I beg leave to let you know that I have read *Common Sense*," Joseph Hawley, one of the senior radicals of Massachusetts, wrote to his fellow patriot Elbridge Gerry, "and that every sentiment has sunk into my well-prepared heart." George Washington himself noted that "*Common Sense* is working a powerful change in the minds of men." Apparently, the change was working on the General himself because he stopped toasting the King at official meals. While John Adams deplored Paine's superficial and naive political theorizing, he recognized the power of the tract and welcomed its effect in solidifying sentiment for independence. When it appeared in Philadelphia, he sent a copy—of course—to Abigail, and to a number of friends and relatives. Deacon Palmer, thanking him, wrote, "I believe no pages was ever more rapturously read, nor more generally approved. People speak of it in rapturous praise." To Joseph Ward it was "a glorious performance," and Abigail Adams, charmed at the writer's sentiments, wondered how "an honest heart, one who wishes the welfare of his country and the happiness of posterity, can hesitate one moment at adopting them."

Common Sense was especially welcomed in New England, where it provoked a flood of letters, petitions and addresses to Congress urging the delegates to declare independence. "This is *the time* for declaring independence," one such correspondent wrote, "we never have had such a favorable moment before, and 'tis not likely we shall have such another if we neglect this." The ordinary people of Massachusetts, James Warren wrote John Adams, "can't account for the hesitancy they observe" in Congress. They wonder why "the dictates of *Common Sense* have not had the same influence upon the enlarged minds of their superiors that they feel on their own, and none can see the safety or happiness in a future connection with Britain, void as [the British] are of true policy, justice or humanity."

The answer, in part, was that it was the very radicalism of *Common Sense*—which seemed to hint at the abolition of all government—that made the more conservative delegates unwilling to cast off the last mooring which bound them all to certainty and security. Warren, on the other hand, believed that "People are as they should be, the harvest is mature. I can't describe the sighing after independence," he added. "It is universal. Nothing remains of that prudence, moderation or timidity with which we have so long been plagued and embarrassed."

The stage was now set. The people in every colony were demanding independence and revolution. The Second Continental Congress was now in session, and even the most reluctant and moderate of the participants felt the pressure of the times. Still, the pace of the proceedings was too slow for many of the delegates. Sam Adams claimed the Congress was turning into "a debating society." His cousin, John, added, "Some people must have time to look around them; before, behind, on the right hand, and on the left; then to think, and, after all this, to resolve." He went on to sigh, "The voice of the representatives is not always consonant with the voice of the people."

But finally, through the efforts of John and Sam Adams, Ben Franklin, and Richard Henry Lee, among others, the breakthrough came. On June 7, 1776, Lee, on behalf of the Virginia delegation, proposed calling the Revolution a revolution, and getting on with winning it. His formal statement—the Virginia Resolution—was a model of simplicity: "Resolved, that these United colonies are, and of right ought to be, free and independent states, and that all political connection between them and the state of Britain is, and ought to be, totally dissolved." While the resolution was argued back and forth between the radicals and the declining group of moderates ("Their moderation," scowled Sam Adams, "has brought us to this pass; and if they were to be regarded, they would continue the conflict a century."), the Congress appointed a five-man committee to frame a declaration in conformity with the Virginia Resolution.

And so, after ten years of organizing, theorizing and agitating; after years in which the mon-

A LIST of the Names of the PROVINCIALS who were Killed and Wounded in the late Engagement with His Majesty's Troops at *Concord*, &c.

KILLED.

Of *Lexington*.
* Mr. Robert Munroe,
* Mr. Jonas Parker,
* Mr. Samuel Hadley,
* Mr. Jonaᵗ Harrington,
* Mr. Caleb Harrington,
* Mr. Isaac Muzzy,
* Mr. John Brown,
Mr. John Raymond,
Mr. Nathaniel Wyman,
Mr. Jedediah Munroe.

Of *Menotomy*.
Mr. Jason Ruffel,
Mr. Jabez Wyman,
Mr. Jason Winship,

Of *Sudbury*.
Deacon Haynes,
Mr. —— Reed.

Of *Concord*.
Capt. James Miles.

Of *Beaford*.
Capt. Jonathan Willson.

Of *Acton*.
Capt. Davis,
Mr. —— Hofmer,
Mr. James Howard.

Of *Woburn*.
* Mr. Azael Porter,
Mr. Daniel Thompson.

Of *Charlestown*.
Mr. James Miller,
Capt. William Barber's Son.

Of *Brookline*.
Isaac Gardner, Esq;

Of *Cambridge*.
Mr. John Hicks,
Mr. Moses Richardson,
Mr. William Massey.

Of *Medford*.
Mr. Henry Putnam.

Of *Lynn*.
Mr. Abednego Ramsdell,
Mr. Daniel Townsend,
Mr. William Flint,
Mr. Thomas Hadley.

Of *Danvers*.
Mr. Henry Jacobs,
Mr. Samuel Cook,
Mr. Ebenezer Goldthwait,
Mr. George Southwick,
Mr. Benjamin Daland, jun.
Mr. Jotham Webb,
Mr. Perley Putnam.

Of *Salem*.
Mr. Benjamin Peirce.

WOUNDED.

Of *Lexington*.
Mr. John Robbins,
Mr. John Tidd,
Mr. Solomon Peirce,
Mr. Thomas Winship,
Mr. Nathaniel Farmer,
Mr. Joseph Comee,
Mr. Ebenezer Munroe,
Mr. Francis Brown,
Prince Eafterbrooks,
  (A Negro Man.

Of *Framingham*.
Mr. —— Hemenway.

Of *Bedford*.
Mr. John Lane.

Of *Woburn*.
Mr. George Reed,
Mr. Jacob Bacon.

Of *Medford*.
Mr. William Polly.

Of *Lynn*.
Joshua Feit,
Mr. Timothy Munroe.

Of *Danvers*.
Mr. Nathan Putnam,
Mr. Dennis Wallis.

Of *Beverly*.
Mr. Nathaniel Cleaves.

MISSING.

Of *Menotomy*.
Mr. Samuel Frost,
Mr. Seth Ruffell.

Thofe diftinguifhed with this Mark [*] were killed by the firft fire of the Regulars

Sold in Queen Street.

G. Tisdale A.b.   d. fculp!—

The TORY'S Day of JUDGMENT.

archy subverted the rights of Americans; after a decade of developing a revolutionary philosophy of government and a new vision of what it could mean to be a human being; after all of these things—an American statement of revolution, the Declaration of Independence, came to be formally written down.

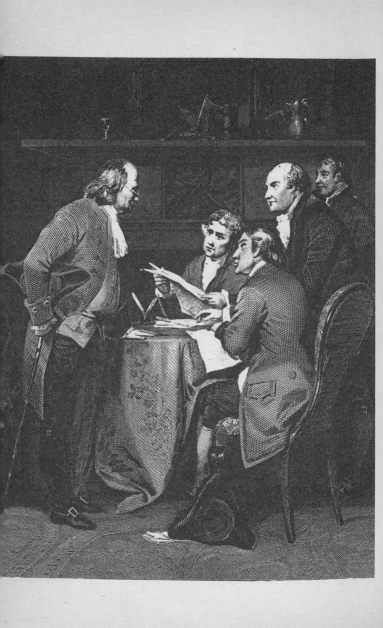

THE DECLARATION OF INDEPENDENCE

The members of the Committee called upon to draft the Declaration were: Thomas Jefferson, John Adams, Benjamin Franklin, Roger Sherman, and Robert Livingston. Jefferson was to be chairman; at age 33, he was one of the youngest members of the Congress. He said very little in the debates at Independence Hall, although he was an ardent patriot. He was not a skillful or effective speaker—but in pamphlets and documents he had written before 1776 he had gained the admiration of many for his clear thinking and what was called his "felicity of language." In short, like Tom Paine, he knew how to turn a phrase.

Jefferson was assigned the work of drafting the statement which was to explain and justify to the world and succeeding generations the action Americans took to declare independence from the English monarchy. His appointed task, as he saw it, was "not to find out new principles, or new arguments, but to place before mankind the common sense of the subject, in terms so plain and firm as to command their assent." The Declaration was to be, he wrote, "an expression of the American mind." Years later he explained

53

to a friend that he consulted not books or high-flung theories in his effort; he had only "looked into the hearts of the people and found it indelibly inscribed there."

The Declaration is really a statement in two parts. The first outlines the democratic theory of government and the right to revolution; the second records the grievances against the King. It is this first part that states the philosophical basis behind the American struggle.

> We hold these truths to be self-evident, That all men are created equal, that they are endowed by their creator with certain un-alienable rights; that among these are life, liberty and the pursuit of happiness; that to secure these rights governments are instituted among men, deriving their just powers from the consent of the governed; that whenever any form of government becomes destructive of these ends, it is the right of the people to alter or to abolish it, and to institute new government, laying its foundation on such principles and organizing its power in such form as to them shall seem most likely to effect their safety and happiness.

Contained within that one statement are three concepts about the individual and society that were the foundation of the patriotism of 1776.

1. *Self-evident truths and inalienable rights.* Jefferson looked back for the justification of the American Revolution not just into the experiences of the colonists, but into the entire history of humanity. Throughout the ages and in all countries, he found, there have been certain rights that all people have either enjoyed or fought to gain. These are birthrights and cannot be nullified by kings, legislators, or any other institution—political, economic, religious or social. To violate these sacred and timeless principles is to stand in

opposition to humanity and to the creator.

The first self-evident truth is that "all men are created equal." This was a very new idea. But as with the other principles in the Declaration, it was the vigor with which Americans pressed for concrete economic and political equality as the Revolution got under way that gave the phrase concrete meaning.

The second of the Declaration's self-evident truths is that every individual is endowed with certain God-given rights, among which are "life, liberty and the pursuit of happiness." The right of all to life had generally been accepted long before the Revolution, but the right of the non-titled and non-wealthy to liberty was new, and the right to the pursuit of happiness was something else again. The phrase first proposed for the Declaration had been "life, liberty and property," but this, it was decided, generally meant preserving things as they are (which, in turn, generally meant that the people with the most property refused to share it with those who had little or none). It was because the delegates, and specifically Jefferson, were unwilling to compromise their vision of the New World, that the phrase was changed. Had the Revolution been just an "independence" movement, "life, liberty and property" might have been sufficient. But this was a revolutionary movement, and to the radical patriots that meant not just breaking away from the monarchical system, but insuring that both political and economic democracy were the cornerstones of the new nation. By asserting that the pursuit of happiness was the right of *all* people, the Declaration proclaimed that a grim life of weary toil was not the only possible destiny. This new vision of humanity's potential was radically different from the Old World view. Acknowledging the "pursuit of happiness" as a God-given right propelled the Americans beyond the concept of independence to one of revolution.

Thomas Jefferson

2. *The purpose of government is to secure the basic human rights, safety and happiness of the people.* Not only was the government supposed to safeguard the people—the traditional role of feudal governments and their armies—but it was also to secure their rights. This was a forward-looking vision, one that spoke, again, of the dawning of a new age, with greater opportunities and hope.

3. *The right of the people to alter or abolish their government.* This was perhaps the most important statement contained within the Declaration, not only for the Americans of 1776, but for succeeding generations as well. It was really an extension of the argument Tom Paine had used in *Common Sense:* people make governments and institutions; people can end or change them.

For a long time, philosophers had debated the question of whether blind obedience was due to kings (the monarch having a "Divine Right" to rule), or whether the people had the right to resist tyrannical rulers. The proponents of this latter notion took as their motto, "*Vox populi, vox dei*": "the voice of the people is the voice of God."

But for the first time, the question of the right of the people to rebel was taken out of the hands of the philosophers. The Declaration made this people's right the basis for the founding of the new nation. It was this idea that sent a shudder through royal courts around the world: what monarch would ever be safe, aristocrats wondered, if this radical notion caught on? The most important thing about the idea, as many saw it, was that by placing the concept in our founding document, Americans of all succeeding generations were granted the same right as their founding ancestors: the right to alter or abolish their government. Fearing that even the new nation might one day stray from the path of democracy, Jefferson tried to guarantee that if tyranny ever

BLISHED BY CURRIER & IVES

Entered according to act of Congress in the year 1876 b

THOMAS JEFFERSON.   ROGER SHERMAN.

THE DECLARA

ives, in the Office of the Librarian of Congress at Washington.

125 NASSAU ST. NEW

IN FRANKLIN.   ROBERT R. LIVINGSTON.   JOHN ADAMS.

N COMMITTEE.

again reared its head over America, posterity would have formal justification for confronting it. In a later part of the Declaration Jefferson went even further. Not only is it the right of the people to revolt against arbitrary, undemocratic rule, he wrote, but it is "the duty" of every patriotic American to do so.

To these three principles of democracy, the fifty-six delegates to the Continental Congress then pledged their "lives, fortunes and sacred honors." Patriots throughout the country also dedicated themselves to these ideals.

To strengthen the case of the Americans against English domination, Jefferson then listed eighteen grievances—"A history of repeated injuries and usurpations," he called them, "all having in direct object the establishment of an absolute tyranny over these States." Some of these indictments against the King were particularly scathing:

> He has refused his assent to laws, the most wholesome and necessary for the public good.

> He has made judges dependent on his will alone, for the tenure of their offices, and the amount and payment of their salaries.

> He has erected a multitude of new offices, and sent hither swarms of officers to harrass our people, and eat out their substance.

> He has kept among us, in times of peace, standing armies without consent of our legislatures.

> He has affected to render the military independent of and superior to the civil power.

> He has combined with others to subject us to a jurisdiction foreign to our constitution, and unacknowledged by our laws; giving his assent to their acts of pretended legislation.

Jefferson ended the list of grievances with an eloquent denunciation:

> In every stage of these oppressions we have petitioned for redress in the most humble terms: our repeated petitions have been answered only by repeated injury. A prince, whose character is thus marked by every act which may define a tyrant, is unfit to be the ruler of a free people.

Jefferson's indictments against George III, like Tom Paine's *Common Sense*, are a classic piece of propaganda. There are no half-way points in a revolution, the grievances proclaim; either we are one hundred percent against the monarchy and all it represents, or we must be willing to live under the King and all the evils that involves. To counter the moderates' continued insistence that there was at least some small measure of benefit from the system of royal government, the radical patriots used the indictments to make the case that reform was impossible. The list of grievances was so extensive that the remaining reformers and apologists for the King found themselves confronted by a dilemma: how can such "abuses and usurpations" be redressed unless the King gives up the power to commit them? In other words, the case against the monarch was made so complete that the *only* way out for Americans appeared to be revolution.

Jefferson's condemnation of the King was so absolute that it even appears to have impressed the King. Years later, after the Americans had successfully completed the war, Adams and Jefferson went to London to meet with their ex-monarch. When told that the author of the Declaration of Independence was in the palace, King George locked himself in his bed chamber and refused to come out.

THE DECLARATION IS APPROVED

Even as Jefferson readied the Declaration for approval by the Congress, the debate over Richard Henry Lee's resolution of independence dragged on inside Independence Hall. Finally, on July 2, 1776, after months of debate, arm-twisting, compromises, and much high-pressured politicking, the vote on the Virginia Resolution—"that these colonies are, and of right, ought to be free and independent states"—was taken and unanimously approved. On July 3, John Adams noted the historic moment in a letter to his wife: "Yesterday the greatest question was decided which ever was decided in America, and a greater, perhaps, never was nor will be decided among men."

Once finished with the formal resolution of independence, the delegates quickly moved to the matter of the Declaration. Jefferson's original version remained virtually intact, with one notable exception. The most damning indictment against King George, one condemning him for fostering the slave trade in America—"He has waged cruel war against human nature itself, violating its most sacred rights of life and liberty in the persons of a distant people who never offended him, captivating and carrying them into

Reading of the Declaration

slavery in another hemisphere . . ."—was struck.
Some of the Southern delegations simply refused
to sign the Declaration unless the deletion was
made, while many others from the North realized
that they were not particularly innocent in the
whole sordid matter either: Northern merchants
were the principal transporters of blacks from
Africa to the Southern plantations. Needing the
unqualified support of all the colonies to wage the
Revolution successfully, the Congress sacrificed
the passage. But the message of equality and inalienable rights still rang out in the Declaration,
and generations of abolitionists and suffragists
were to later base their own movements for justice on the "self-evident" truths of our founding
document.

Finally, on July 4, the debate over, the vote
was taken and the Declaration of Independence
was approved. It was a bold step, and a treason-
ous one in the eyes of the King, one ranking right

at the top of offenses against the Crown punishable by death.

The men who signed the Declaration realized that from that moment on they were hunted criminals. Benjamin Rush recalled that they had all signed "with a noose around our necks." Ben Franklin replied, half in humor, half in deadly earnest: "Yes, we must all hang together, or we shall all hang separately." Abraham Clark, a delegate from New Jersey, who had won fame by fighting for poor and working people in court, dryly noted, "Perhaps our Congress will be exalted on a high gallows." When little Elbridge Gerry of Massachusetts went to the table to sign, portly Benjamin Harrison of Virginia remarked, "When we hang for what we're doing, from the size and weight of my body, I'll die quickly; but you're so light, you'll swing in the air for hours before you're dead." It was a big gamble these men were taking, and the stakes were the highest possible. Understandably, John Adams wrote, "Several signed with regret and several others with many doubts." But if some of the men who signed the Declaration had misgivings, people throughout the country showed enthusiastic support for the revolutionary document. Like *Common Sense*, the Declaration of Independence was read and discussed around the new nation.

It's first public reading came on July 8 in Philadelphia. John Nixon, a patriot leader in the city, stood in the State House yard and read the document to a crowd which (according to a Tory observer) contained "very few respectable people." John Adams observed the celebration that followed: "Three cheers rended the welkin. The batallions paraded on the Common and gave us a *feu-de-joie*, notwithstanding the scarcity of powder. The bells rang all day and almost all night."

Other demonstrations of support soon followed

Removing the King's arms from the Boston State House

in other cities. In New York, General Washington had the Declaration read to his assembled troops, and followed it with a typically terse proclamation to his men:

> The General hopes that this important event will serve as a fresh incentive to every officer and soldier to act with fidelity and courage, as knowing that now the peace and safety of his country depends solely on the success of our arms.

Later in the day, the citizens of New York, along with a great many of the General's troops, assembled on the Bowling Green to hear the Declaration read again. With the last words, a cheer went up and the crowd marched off to a gilt-covered lead statue of King George atop his horse. A New York newspaper gave this account of the event:

> Tonight the equestrian statue of George III has, by the Sons of Freedom, been laid prostrate in the dirt—the just desert of an ungrateful tyrant! The lead wherewith the

monument was made is to be run into bullets to assimilate with the brains of our infatuated adversaries.

Abigail Adams recorded events in Boston: "The bells rang, the privateers fired the forts and batteries, the cannon were discharged and every fact appeared joyful . . . After dinner, the king's arms were taken down from the State House and every vestige of him from every place . . . and burnt . . . Thus ends royal authority in this State, and all the people shall say Amen." Her friend and fellow revolutionary, James Warren, added, "Every one of us feels more important than ever. We now congratulate each other as freemen."

The tone was different, but no less patriotic, in Savannah, Georgia, where King George was buried in a mock funeral oration:

> We commit his political existence to the ground—corruption to corruption—tyranny to the grave—and oppression to eternal infamy, in sure and certain hope that he will never obtain a resurrection, to rule again over the United States of America.

The celebrations continued, even as Americans prepared for war. At the end of July a child in East Windsor, Connecticut, was baptized Independence.

THE DECLARATION IN ACTION: AT HOME

The story of the Declaration of Independence really only begins with the signing and the first celebrations in its honor. The reason that the Declaration is one of the world's most important statements of human rights and revolution is simply because it was more than a document. It became a living tradition.

In their own day, the signers of the Declaration saw its revolutionary principles become a prescription for action, both in this country and abroad. Indeed, some of the founders who had hoped the Declaration would be no more than a statement of separation from England grew alarmed at the implications of the document. Right from the beginning, our first politicians learned that it is easy to mouth praise for democratic ideals; but difficulties arise when people decide to put those ideals into practice. Hardly had the fireworks and parades ended when Americans began to see what the Revolution could mean in their day-to-day lives.

The first use made of the Declaration to further the Revolution here at home was against those feudal codes—primogeniture, entail, and quit-rents—which had allowed vast concentrations of

economic power to get into the hands of a few. The codes were remnants of the feudal system of the Old World that had made their way to America over one hundred years before. Now, the patriots argued, if all people were really equal, with *equal* rights to life, liberty and the pursuit of happiness, then they all must start with the same chance in life. The attack was not, of course, launched at *all* private property; property was a good thing, Jefferson claimed, so good in fact, that everybody should have a little, and nobody should have a great deal. Benjamin Franklin, writing with the clarity and common sense he was famous for, explained the distinction between that "private property" necessary for human survival, and those "concentrations of property" that would lead the new nation back into despotism:

> All the property that is necessary to a man for the conservation of the individual, and the propagation of the species, is his natural right which none can justly deprive him of; but all property superfluous to such purposes is the property of the public who, by their laws have created it, and who may, therefore, by other laws dispose of it, whenever the welfare of the public shall desire such disposition.

It was against these concentrations of "superfluous" property that the patriots turned the new nation's first principles of economic democracy.

The new state legislatures, now in the hands of the patriots, began the assault on the feudal codes. Three months after drafting the Declaration, Jefferson was back in the Virginia House of Delegates. Within a week he submitted a bill to overturn the entail system and to break up large estates. (Entail restricted the passage of property to an owner's lineal descendants.) Conservative opposition was quickly overwhelmed, and over half the area of Virginia was released from the large landholders.

THE HORSE AN

Pub.^d as the Act directs, Aug.st 1.st 1779

ERICA, *throwing his Master.*

White, Angel Court, Westminster.

Quitrents (feudal taxes paid by poor farmers to the owners of the huge estates) were still in force in many areas of America up to 1776. These were swept away. Primogeniture (the custom of passing on an estate to the oldest son) had been especially strong in New York and the South before the Revolution. Now, it too was abolished. Landholdings belonging to Tories were confiscated and redistributed at generous terms to patriots to help finance the war. At the same time, the new revolutionary state governments came to the aid of poor debtors by printing large quantities of paper money with which they could pay their bills. The revolutionaries realized, that there was still a long way to go toward real economic democracy, but the unprecedented assault on these large property holdings and concentrations of wealth was a suitable start.

The patriots also turned their democratic principles on concentrations of *political power*. Even before the Declaration was approved, royal authority in virtually every area of the country was at an end. With the coming of the Revolution, the thirteen states began to form their own constitutions. The founders had always distrusted power, and viewed George III as but the latest example of what could happen when all the power in a society was placed in one man. Accordingly these new constitutions were written so that state power was diffused as much as possible. The newly constituted legislatures which (in early theory at least) were to be the most direct representatives of the people, were given all the executive power and authority that had formerly rested in the royal governor alone. In North Carolina, as the new constitution was debated, one delegate to the convention was asked what power the governor would have in this new democratic system. "The power to sign a receipt for his salary," he answered. The Meckenburg County delegation to this same convention was instructed by the people to seek "a simple democracy, or as near it as possible. Oppose everything that leans to aristocracy of power in the hands of the rich and chief men exercised to the oppression of the poor."

The attack on undemocratic political power continued. In New Hampshire, the eastern Establishment announced an electoral plan that neglected to give representation to the working people in the western part of the state. In response, the people of Grafton County, led by professors at a small college, refused to hold elections and announced that the constitutional assembly had made itself illegitimate. "We conceive that the power of government reverted to the people at large," a delegation of the county wrote, "and of course annihilated the political existence of the assembly." In Virginia, the small farmers of the western part of that State arrayed themselves against the remains of the old-line gentry of Williamsburg. When they finally defeated the gentry in politics, they flaunted their victory by transferring the capital from chic Williamsburg to the west, where they could keep an eye on it.

The revolutionary movement also sparked a call from the people for bills of rights. By the end of the war, many of the new state constitutions included a formal enumeration of the rights of citizens, setting a precedent for the Federal Constitution when it was drafted twenty years later. Virginia was the first to approve a bill of rights. Much of the revolutionary philosophy of the Declaration was included in it. Among the principles it listed were:

That all people are created equal; that power is vested in and derives from the people; that government is instituted for the benefit, security and protection of the people; that elections should be free and open to all members of the community; that all laws must be approved by the representatives of the people; that excessive bail or fines should not be imposed, nor cruel and unusual punishment inflicted; that standing armies in times of peace are dangerous; that freedom of press and religion are guaranteed.

The Virginia Bill of Rights ended by articulating the basic assumptions implicit in the Revolution: "That no free government, or the blessings of liberty can be preserved to any people, but by a firm adherence to justice, moderation, temperance, frugality and virtue, and by frequent recurrence to fundamental principles."

Democratic changes were taking place on all levels of society. Reforms of the criminal codes and penal systems were demanded and acted on by the revolutionaries. Moderates accused the radicals of being soft on crime, but the radicals pointed out that no one was harder on crime than they were, when the crime was against democratic principles. In Virginia, the death penalty was abolished for all but two crimes, one of them being treason; treason was defined by Jefferson's friend, John Taylor, as "giving power to an aristocracy."

Women were playing a major part in the war. Many were members of organizations like the Daughters of Liberty, who worked in support of front-line troops. In some cases women even took up arms in battle. As a result, women began to demand the fulfillment of the promise of equality for themselves. It was slow in coming, but there were some unheard of advances for the times. With the passage of the Declaration, women in New Jersey gained the right to vote alongside men. (In 1807, with the principles of the Revolu-

Molly Pitcher

Nancy Hart

Mrs. Schyler burning her wheat fields as the British approach

tion apparently growing dim, New Jersey took their vote away.) Abigail Adams, writing to her husband while the vote on Independence was still being debated, struck a tone that still reverberates today when she warned her husband that women were going to take the principles of equality seriously.

While you are proclaiming peace and good
will to men, emancipating all nations, you
insist upon retaining an absolute power over
wives . . . In the new code of laws which I
suppose will be necessary for you to make,
I desire that you would remember the ladies
and be more generous and favorable to them
than your ancestors. Do not put such unlimited power into the hands of the husbands.
Remember, all men would be tyrants if they
could. If particular care and attention is not
paid to the ladies, we are determined to
foment a rebellion, and will not hold ourselves bound by any laws in which we have
no voice or representation.

Black people, too, began demanding that the
promise of equality be made good. Although
the passage on the slave trade was struck from
the list of "abuses and usurpations," many of the
revolutionaries attacked the practice of slavery
in their state legislatures. During and shortly
after the Revolution, the slave trade was pro-
hibited or heavily taxed in eleven states. Massachusetts and New Hampshire abolished slavery
altogether. Like women, blacks found a gap between the promise of equality and the reality of
American life; like women, black people have continued to demand that America honor its
Declaration.

By the time the war was over in 1783, radical
American patriots agreed that while there was
still a long way to go in the fight to make the
Declaration's democratic vision a living reality,
an important beginning had been made. And
while they did not expect to finish the job in their
lifetime, the founders were optimistic that succeeding generations of Americans would carry
the struggle forward.

THE DECLARATION
IN ACTION: ABROAD

The principles of the Declaration of Independence were not the sole property of Americans, nor were they aimed just at the tyranny of King George III. The principles were universal, they belonged to all people, and they were aimed at tyranny everywhere. From the first, the Spirit of '76 attracted world-wide attention: excitement and hope in foreign radicals; fear and loathing in foreign monarchs.

Even before the beginning of our own Revolution, Americans had observed and supported radicals in other nations. Patriots in this country held huge rallies in support of the English radical John Wilkes, when Wilkes was jailed for publishing pamphlets criticizing the Government. Americans were also staunch supporters of the Corsican insurrectionist, Pasquale Paoli, who fought to rid his country of Italian domination. The *New York Journal* hailed him as "the greatest man on earth," and went on to add that the Corsican struggle was "extremely interesting to every friend of liberty and the just rights of mankind." In 1768, the Liberty Tree of Providence, Rhode Island was dedicated "in the name and behalf of all the true Sons of Liberty in America, Great

Britain, Ireland, Corsica, or wheresoever they may be dispersed throughout the world."

With the coming of our own Revolution Americans found they were suddenly in the forefront of the worldwide democratic movement. Foreign radicals were eager to come to America to aid in the struggle here and take back the experiences and principles they found in the new nation to help in the liberation of their own country. Tom Paine, of course, came from England; the Marquis de Lafayette, Baron de Kalb, and Comte de Rochambeau from France; Thaddeus Kosciusko and Casimir Pulaski from Poland; Alexander and Demetrios Ypsilanti from Greece. When the American war was over, many of these foreign-born radicals went back to their native countries to foment their own revolutions. Lafayette was present at the storming of the Bastille by the Paris mob; Kosciusko stirred up several rebellions against Russian interference in his native Poland.

At the same time the foreign revolutionaries carried the message of the Declaration back to their own countries, many of America's own radicals travelled abroad and found vast audiences for their new democratic ideas. In France, Benjamin Franklin noted that the hopes of the people could be boiled down to a simple formula, "Liberty, Equality, Fraternity"; soon the words were coming from the massed throats of the French mob. John Adams travelled to Holland and propagandized about the new revolutionary era that would sweep the world; before long, Dutch patriots were calling for *Vrijheid en Gelijkheit* (liberty and equality). Militant Belgian radicals followed the example of the French and Dutch and pressed for constitutions like those of the most democratic American states. The province of Flanders even declared its independence from the Dutch in the words of the American Declaration.

Prince Radischev of Russia visited America to view this new idea of democracy in action. Upon returning to his native land, he published a poem composed in honor of the American Revolution: "Ode to Liberty." In it he praised the new state constitutions, Pennsylvania's penal laws, and our Revolution in general. The Empress, Catherine the Great, sent him to Siberia. Radischev is still regarded as the first Russian revolutionary.

Europe was not the only hotbed of radicalism. While the Revolution in our part of North America proceeded, the great South American revolutionary, Tupuc Amaru, led a rebellion against the Spanish Aristocrats that was fought across southern Peru, Argentina and Bolivia. After our war was over, South American radicals approached Jefferson for support for their continuing struggle.

Even the English radicals took inspiration from the Revolution that the Declaration launched. At a birthday party for Charles James Fox, King George's bitterest British critic, the Duke of Norfolk, told the assembled throng, "The illustrious George Washington had not more than two thousand men to rally around him when his country was attacked. America is now free. This day full two thousand men are assembled in this place."

Tom Paine, who ranked right at the top of King George's hate list for his sweeping denunciation of the monarch in *Common Sense,* couldn't resist the temptation of returning to England and joining with the English radicals at stirring up rebellion. He soon found himself writing once more, this time in rebuttal to an anti-revolutionary work by Edmund Burke called *Reflections on the French Revolution.* Paine's counter-attack, *The Rights of Man,* was hailed by the poor of London and viciously denounced

The Storming and taking the BASTILE

y the Citizens of PARIS, 14ᵗʰ July, 1789.

by the Tories, who feared it might prove to be the *Common Sense* of England. Paine barely escaped imprisonment for his energetic efforts at fomenting rebellion by fleeing to France. There he met up with his old friend, Lafayette, who presented him with the key to the Bastille to take back to America for George Washington.

Thomas Jefferson was in France at the same time. As America's Ambassador to the country, he had witnessed first-hand the French Revolution. Jefferson was disturbed that the excesses of the guillotine would obscure the real issues of the conflict, and so, in an attempt to win sympathy for the French cause in particular, and continuing revolutions in general, he wrote an impassioned defense of the rebellion:

> In the struggle which was necessary, many guilty persons fell without the form of trial, and with them some innocent. These I deplore as much as anybody, and shall deplore some of them to the day of my death. But I deplore them as I should have done had they fallen in battle. It was necessary to use the arm of the people—a machine not quite so blind as cannon balls and bombs, but blind to a certain degree. A few of their cordial friends met at their hands the fate of enemies. But a time and truth will rescue and embalm their memories, while their posterity will be enjoying that very liberty for which they would never have hesitated to offer up their lives. The liberty of the whole earth was depending on the issue of the contest. And was ever a prize won with so *little* innocent blood? My own affections have been deeply wounded by some of the martyrs to this cause, but rather than it should have failed, I would have seen half the earth desolated. And were there but an Adam and an Eve left in every country, it would be better than it now is.

Many of the revolutions of the 18th Century failed. Others, like the French, ended in the collapse of the revolutionary ideals, and the takeover by military dictators. But the vision of a new life and new hope stayed with the people, to be resurrected at some future day. Years later, on July 4, 1826—the 50th anniversary of the Declaration of Independence that he wrote—Thomas Jefferson issued his last statement to his fellow Americans, affirming in his final breath the Revolution that had begun so long before:

Our fellow citizens, after half a century of experience and prosperity, continue to approve the choice we made. May it be to the world what I believe it will be (to some parts sooner, to others later, but finally to all) the signal of arousing men to burst the chains under which monkish ignorance and superstition had persuaded them to bind themselves, and to assume the blessings and security of self-government. The form which we have substituted restores the free right to the unbounded exercise of reason and freedom of opinion. All eyes are opened, or opening to the rights of man. The general spread of the light of science has already laid open to every view the palpable truth that the mass of mankind has not been born with saddles on their backs, nor a favored few booted and spurred, ready to ride them legitimately, by the grace of God. These are the grounds of hope for others. For ourselves, let the annual return of this day forever refresh our recollections of these rights, and an undiminished devotion to them.

Benjamin Rush

THE LIVING DECLARATION TODAY

In 1787—eleven years after the Declaration and four years after the end of the Revolutionary War, Benjamin Rush said: "The American war is over, but this is far from the case with the American Revolution. On the contrary, only the first act of the great drama is at a close."

At the Constitutional Convention, Benjamin Franklin was asked what kind of a government the new nation would have. "A republic," he replied, "*if* you can keep it." He might just as well have been speaking to us today. Our generation, like the revolutionary generation of two centuries ago, stands at a crucial point in history. Our ancestors opened this great drama when they dared to stand up to the King and all the entrenched wealth and power he represented. People all over the world looked to America to see the great experiment in democracy and revolution that unfolded here.

Americans of other generations continued that drama. Abolitionists, suffragists, the early labor organizers, progressive farmers, civil rights activists—all took the democratic ideals of our Revolution to heart and used them to continue the revolutionary tradition.

And what of our generation of Americans? Are we to continue to be strangers in our own land; to continue to be unaware, even afraid of the principles that founded this country? Were Jefferson to look into our hearts today, what would he find there? A people so removed from their own democratic birthrights that they regard the document he wrote as a pile of "Commie junk"? If this is what we Americans of the 1970s are content to be, then we deserve the biting words of Sam Adams:

> If you love wealth better than liberty, the tranquility of servitude better than the animating contest of freedom, go home from us in peace. Crouch down and lick the hands which feed you. May your chains set lightly upon you, and may posterity forget that you were our countrymen.

Turn and twist which way we will, the simple fact is that this country was born in revolution, and dedicated to democratic principles that pitted us against all the entrenched forces of reaction both at home and abroad. It was our country's earliest hope and pride that it might in turn give birth to many more revolutions designed to free people everywhere from tyranny and oppression. We Americans of today must come to grips with the principles of that first Revolution of two hundred years ago. The great drama cries out to be re-opened. Will we stand by, allowing history to sweep our democracy aside? Or will we, like our ancestors, assert ourselves and the power that lies within us, to regain control of our lives and the institutions around us?

Like the founders of this country, we too have lived through turbulent times in our own decades of the '60s and '70s. The scandals and revelations of the past few years have shaken all Americans and our faith in the institutions that shape and govern our Nation. Many of us have even re-signed ourselves to deceit and corruption among our politicians. We have resigned ourselves to the notion that our giant business corporations will continue to buy and sell our elected representatives, will continue to make record profits by fabricating shortages and raising prices, will continue to control our very lives without our consent. It is just this resignation and acceptance that those who would destroy our democratic birthright depend on. If we who believe in the principles of our first revolution do not act, others, who do not believe in them will act for us, taking our silence for cowardice, our despair for acceptance.

We are now in the midst of the Bicentennial of the American Revolution, a period that will extend into the 1980s. Like our ancestors two hundred years ago, we must all go to school again in the principles of democracy and make this a time of questioning, of choice, and of action on the vital issues of today. The questions we must answer by actions are clear:

- How can we insure that massive corruption and contempt for the democratic principles of 1776 will no longer find a home in the highest levels of our Government?
- How can we return to the principles of economic democracy, and stand up to the giant corporations that represent unelected and undemocratic concentrations of power and wealth?
- How can we resurrect our original revolutionary views that propelled us into the forefront of the world-wide democratic movement?

These questions, and others, are the crucial ones we all face as Americans. The time for pomp and circumstance and vague platitudes about democracy is ending. It is time to relive our Revolution. It is time to relearn the lessons of our history; to refer back again to our first principles. The Declaration of Independence, as our founding document, is the door through which we must pass in order to arm ourselves with the knowledge and power that our first rebellion against tyranny offers us. Beyond that, we must look more closely at what this country was designed to be. What did our first revolutionaries think of the institutions of this Nation—our military, our political leaders, our banks and corporations? What did they think of the people, and of our ability to govern ourselves and control our own destinies?

What follows are more than quotations. They are universal principles of democracy in whose name a revolution was fought. It's time we take them as seriously as did our founders. Their words are our words.

Voices From
The American Revolution

THE PEOPLE

THE CITIZEN IN A DEMOCRACY

What do we mean by the Revolution? The war? That was no part of the Revolution: it was only an effect and consequence of it. The Revolution was in the minds of the people, and this was effected, from 1760 to 1775, in the course of fifteen years before a drop of blood was shed at Lexington.

John Adams, 1815

The PEOPLE, I say, are the only competent judges of their own welfare.

Josiah Quincy, 1774

May nothing ever check that glorious spirit of freedom which inspires the patriot in the cabinet, and the hero in the field, with courage to maintain their righteous cause, and to endeavor to transmit the claim to posterity, conveyance to their children with their blood.

> Mercy Warren, 1788

Wherever public spirit prevails, liberty is secure.

> Noah Webster, 1764

Were governments to offer freedom to the people, or show an anxiety for that purpose, the offer most probably would be rejected. The purpose for which it was offered might be mistrusted. Therefore the desire to originate with and proceed from the mass of the people; and when the impression becomes universal, and not before, is the important moment for the most effectual consolidation of national strength and greatness that can take place.

> Tom Paine, 1795

The origin of all power is in the people, and . . . they have an incontestible right to check the creatures of their own creation.

> Mercy Warren, 1788

The high things that are said in favor of rulers and of their dignitaries, and upon the side of power, will not be able to stop people's mouths when they feel themselves oppressed.

> Andrew Hamilton, 1735

The moral sense is as much a part of our Constitution as that of feeling, seeing or hearing; as a wise Creator must have seen to be necessary in an animal destined to live in society; that every human mind feels pleasure in doing good to another.

> Thomas Jefferson, 1815

It is a maxim that in every government, there must exist somewhere, a supreme, sovereign, absolute, and uncontrollable power; but this power resides always in the body of the people; and it never was, or can be, delegated to one man or a few; the Creator has never given to men a right to vest others with authority over them, unlimited either in duration or degree.

Proclamation of the General
Court of Massachusetts, 1776

If it be asked, who are the proper judges to determine when rulers are guilty of tyranny and oppression, I answer, the public.

Samuel West, 1776

Let the colonies still convince their implacable enemies that they are united in constitutional principles, and are resolved they *will not* be slaves; that their dependence is not upon merchants or any particular class of men.

Sam Adams, 1770

Public opinion sets the bounds to every government and is the real sovereign of every free one.

Philip Freneau, 1791

I know very well that it has been handed about as a political creed of late, that the reasoning of the "people without doors" is not to be regarded. But every "transient person" has a right publicly to criticize upon whatever is publicly advanced by any man; and I am resolved to exercise that right when I please, without asking any man's leave.

Sam Adams, 1770

When once it appears beyond contradiction that we are united in sentiments, there will be a confidence in each other, and a plan of opposition will be easily formed and executed with spirit.

Sam Adams, 1772

There is very little difference in that superstition which leads us to believe in what the world calls *great men*, and in that which leads us to believe in witches and conjurors.

Benjamin Rush, 1808

(The Government of King George says) that this great Revolution has been the work of a faction, of a junto of ambitious men against the sense of the people of America. On the contrary, nothing has been done without the approbation of the people, who have indeed outrun their leaders, so that no capital measure has been adopted until they called loudly for it.

George Mason, 1778

In vain 'tis for some few (and very few I hope they are) who, governed either by base principles of fear, or led by vile hopes of gain, the reward of prostituted virtue, to say, "your rights are indeed invaded, but Great Britain is too strong. What can we do against superior strength?" Let these evil designing men remember that the highest authority has told us, "that the race is not always to the swift nor the battle to the strong." The truth is that all nations are furnished with the means of defending their natural rights, if they have but wisdom and fortitude to make the proper use of such means.

William Rind, 1769

If the people are at present hushed into silence, is it not a sort of sullen silence, which is far from indicating that the glorious spirit of liberty is vanquished and left without hope but in miracles?

Sam Adams, 1771

Young as you are, the cruel war, into which we have been compelled by the haughty tyrant . . . and the bloody emissaries of his vengence, may stamp upon your minds this certain truth, that the welfare and prosperity of all countries and communities, and, I may add, individuals, depend upon their morals. That nation to which we were once united, as it has departed from justice, eluded and subverted the wise laws, which formerly governed it, and suffered the worst crimes to go unpunished, has lost its valor, wisdom, and humanity, and has sunk into derision and infamy.

Abigail Adams, 1778

God Save the *People*.

Massachusetts Proclamation, 1778

OUR DEMOCRATIC BIRTHRIGHTS

We hold these truths to be self-evident, that all men are created equal, that they are endowed by their creator with certain unalienable rights, that among these are life, liberty, and the pursuit of happiness . . .

The Declaration of Independence, 1776

The sole end of government is protection and security of the people. Whenever, therefore, that power which was originally instituted to effect these important and valuable purposes is employed to harass, distress, or enslave the people, in this case it becomes a curse rather than a blessing.

Provincial Congress of Massachusetts, 1774

Is life so dear, or peace so sweet, as to be purchased at the price of chains and slavery? Forbid it almighty

God! I know not what course others may take, but as for me, give me liberty or give me death!

Patrick Henry, 1775

I am not a beast or a dog, but am a man as well as yourself. Since then human nature agrees equally with all persons; and since no one can live a sociable life with another that does not own or respect him as a man; it follows as a command of the law of nature, that every man esteem and treat another as one who is naturally his equal or who is a man as well as he . . .

John Wise, 1717

Where liberty is, there is my country.

Benjamin Franklin, 1783

Where liberty is not, there is mine.

Tom Paine, 1783

Your life, your liberties, your property, will be at the disposal only of your Creator and yourselves. You will know no power but such as you create, no authority unless derived from your grant; no law, but such as acquires full their obligations from your consent.

John Jay, 1777

It is not property only we contend for. Our liberty and most essential privileges are struck at: arbitrary courts are set over us, the trials by juries taken away, the press is so restricted that we cannot complain, an army of mercenaries threatened to be billeted on us, the source of our trade stopped, and to complete our ruin, the little property we had acquired, taken from us, without even allowing us the merit of giving it. I really dread the consequences.

Charles Thompson, 1765

Ever since I arrived at the state of manhood and acquainted myself with the general history of mankind, I have felt a sincere passion for liberty. The history of nations doomed to perpetual slavery, in consequences of yielding up their natural-born liberties, I read with a philosophical horror; so that the first systematical and bloody attempt, at Lexington, to enslave America, thoroughly electrified my mind, and fully determined me to take part with my country.

Ethan Allen, 1779

Liberté, Egalité, Fraternité.
Ben Franklin's suggestion for a
slogan for the French Revolution

Nothing is more certain than that the *forms* of liberty may be retained, when the substance is gone.
John Dickinson, 1768

It is the form of government which gives the decisive color to the manners of a people more than any other thing.
John Adams, 1776

Preserve America therefore an asylum for the distressed of all nations, and a land of liberty for yourselves. Let the oppressions that forced them, and continually obliges many of the other nations of Europe to leave their native soil, teach you wisdom; let it teach you to value the envied blessings you enjoy, purchased by the perilous toil and stern virtue of your ancestors, therefore leave these blessings which they left you, unimpaired to your posterity. If you suffer the iron rod of oppression to reach and scourge you here, remember you have no America to flee to for asylum. Here you must be free men, or the most abject and mortified slaves. There is no alternative; therefore, stand firm, acquit yourselves like free men, who value liberty and life alike.

Anonymous broadside, 1773

Liberty consists in the power of choosing without danger, without dread.

The Federal Gazette, 1792

Those who are desirous of enjoying all the advantages of liberty themselves, should be willing to extend personal liberty to others.

Rhode Island Assembly, 1774

The natural liberty of man is to be free from any superior power on Earth, and not to be under the will or legislative authority of man, but only to have the law of nature for his rule.

Sam Adams, 1772

Happily, the government of the United States . . . gives to bigotry no sanction, to persecution no assistance.

George Washington, 1790

The present is an age of philosophy, and America the empire of reason. Here, neither the pageantry of courts, nor the glooms of superstition, have dazzled or beclouded the mind. Our duty calls us to act worthy of the age and the country that gave us birth. Though inexperience may have betrayed us into errors—yet they have not been fatal: and our own discernment will point us to their proper remedy.

Joel Barlow, 1787

The rights of individuals ought to be the primary objects of all government, and cannot be too securely guarded by the most explicit declarations in their favor.

Mercy Warren, 1788

PATRIOTISM

All are not dead; and where there is a spark of patriotic fire, we will enkindle it. Say you that the Tories spare no pains to disparage our measures? I knew they would, and should have greatly doubted of the importance of the measures if they had not been much nettled.

Sam Adams, 1772

It is at all times necessary, and more particularly so during the progress of a revolution and until right ideas confirm themselves by habit, that we frequently refresh our patriotism by reference to first principles. It is by tracing things to their origin that we learn to understand them, and it is by keeping that line and that origin always in view that we never forget them. An inquiry into the origin of rights will demonstrate to us that rights are not gifts from one man to another, nor from one class of men to another.

Tom Paine, 1795

Some boast of being friends to government; I am a friend to righteous government founded upon the principles of reason and justice; but I glory in publicly avowing my eternal enmity to tyranny.

John Hancock, 1774

A whole government of our own choice, managed by persons whom we love, revere and can confide in, has charms in it for which men will fight.

John Adams

Real patriots, who may resist the intrigues of the favorite, are liable to become suspected and odious; while its tools and dupes usurp the applause and confidence of the people, to surrender their interests.

> George Washington, Farewell Address, 1796

(The founding principles) should be the creed of our political faith, the text of civic instruction, the touchstone by which to try the services of those we trust; and should we wander from them in moments of error or of alarm, let us hasten to retrace our steps to regain the road which alone leads to peace, liberty, safety.

> Thomas Jefferson, 1807

However unbounded may be the wish of power to extend itself, however unwilling it may be to acknowledge mistakes, 'tis surely the duty of every wise and worthy American to point out all invasions of the public liberty and to show the proper methods of obtaining redress.

> William Rind, 1769

An army of principles will penetrate where an army of soldiers cannot.

> Tom Paine, 1795

They that can give up essential liberty to obtain a little temporary safety deserve neither liberty nor safety.

> Benjamin Franklin, 1759

Is it possible that he whom no moral obligations bind, can have any real goodwill towards man? Can he be a patriot who by an openly vicious conduct is undermining the very bonds of society, corrupting the morals of youth, and, by his bad example, injuring that very country he professes to patronize?

> Abigail Adams, 1775

Every man in a republic is public property. His time and talents—his youth—his manhood—his old age—nay more, his life, his all belong to his country. Patriots of 1774, 1775, 1776—heroes of 1778, 1779, 1780! come forward! Your country demands your services! Hear her proclaiming, in sighs and groans, in her governments, in her finances, in her trade, in her manufactures, in her morals, and in her manners, "The Revolution Is Not Over!"

Benjamin Rush, 1787

I will oppose this tyranny at the threshold, though the fabric of liberty fall, and I perish in its ruins.

Sam Adams (as quoted by his
daughter after his death)

My friends and countrymen—I have observed that some of you are a little surprised that I, with so many inducements as I have to remain at home, should have resolved to quit my family and my farm for the fatigues and dangers of war. I mean you should be perfectly satisfied as to my motives. I am an American: and am determined to be free. I was born free: and have never forfeited my birth-right; nor will I ever, like the infatuated son of Isaac, sell it for a mess of pottage. I will part with my life sooner than my liberty, for I prefer an honorable death to the miserable and despicable existence of a slave.

Speech by a farmer of Philadelphia
upon joining the Continental Army,
1776

Let the history of the Federal Government instruct mankind that the mask of patriotism may be worn to conceal the foulest designs against the liberties of the people.

Benjamin Bache, 1798

Only lay down true principles and adhere to them inflexibly. Do not be frightened into their surrender by the alarms of the timid, or the croakings of wealth against the ascendancy of the people.

Thomas Jefferson, 1816

In perilous times like these, I cannot conceive of prudence without fortitude; and the man who is not resolved to encounter and overcome difficulties when the liberty of his country is threatened no more deserves the character of a patriot than another does that of a soldier who flies from his standard.

Sam Adams, 1771

The man who employs his talents, to direct his countrymen in the path of truth, or guard them against impending evils, is a blessing to his country. But he, who prostitutes his pen, to deceive his neighbors into the dark mazes of error, or to lull their virtuous apprehensions asleep, on a matter of the utmost importance, to their safety, and felicity, is a curse to the community, and a disgrace to human nature.

Broadside, signed "Rusticus," 1773

These are the times that try men's souls; the summer soldier and the sunshine patriot will, in this crisis, shrink from the service of his country; but he that stands it now, deserves the love and thanks of man and woman.

Tom Paine, 1776

Nothing, in my opinion, can convey a more unjust idea of the spirit of a true American than to suppose he would even compliment, much less make an adulating address to, any person sent here to trample on the rights of his country, or that he would ever condescend to kiss the hand which is already prepared to rivet his own fetters.

Sam Adams, 1771

Every good citizen will be inclined from duty as well as interest, to love his country, and to be zealous in advancing its welfare. 'Tis to the exertion of the common good, that he owes the security of his life and property; and he will of course feel himself under an obligation of contributing his share to the promotion of public happiness. The man who makes the general interest of the society, of which he is a member, the prevailing objects of his actions, justly merits the honorable title of a patriot.

> Anonymous broadside, addressed "To the Worthy Inhabitants of New York," 1773

The *true patriot* will enquire into the causes of the fears and jealousies of his countrymen. And if he finds they are not groundless, he will be far from endeavoring to allay or stifle them. On the contrary, constrained by the love of his country and from public views, he will by all proper means in his power *foment* and cherish them. He will, as far as he is able, keep the attention of his fellow citizens awake to their grievances and not suffer them to be at rest til the causes of their just complaints are removed.

> Sam Adams, 1771

I have taken more pains in this cause than I will ever take again, although my engaging in this and another popular cause has raised much resentment. But I think I can sincerely declare that I cheerfully submit myself to every odious name for conscience' sake. And from my soul I despise all those whose guilt, malice or folly has made them my foes. Let the consequences be what they will, I am determined to proceed. The only principles of public conduct that are worthy of a man are to sacrifice estate, ease, health and applause, and even life, to the sacred calls of his country.

> Sam Adams

I remember that during the war of the Revolution, it was a fashionable argument on the British side to say that the Yankees were in rebellion to save three pence a pound in the cost of their tea. But the legislature of Massachusetts of that day never instituted an inquiry *how much* the people of America would have to pay by submitting to the tax. It was "for a principle" as one of our poets said at that time, that the nation bled.

John Quincy Adams

Every state in America has, by the repeated voice of its inhabitants, directed and authorized the Continental Congress to publish a formal declaration of independence of, and separation from, the oppressive King and Parliament of Great Britain: and we look on every man as an enemy who does not, in some line or other, give his assistance towards supporting the same.

Pennsylvania Council of Safety

Guard against the postures of pretended patriotism.
George Washington, 1796

THE RIGHT TO REVOLUTION

That to secure these rights, governments are instituted among men, deriving their just power from the consent of the governed, that whenever any form of government becomes destructive of these ends, it is the right of the people to alter or abolish it, and to institute new government, laying its foundation on such principles, and organizing its powers in such form, as to them shall seem most likely to effect their safety and happiness.

> The Declaration of Independence, 1776

Nature points the path, and our enemies have obliged us to persue it.

> Tom Paine, 1776

This country will be made the field of bloody contention till it gains that independence for which nature formed it. It is, therefore, injustice and cruelty to our offspring, and would stamp us with the character of baseness and cowardice, to leave the salvation of this country to be worked out by them with accumulated difficulty and danger.

> Sam Adams, 1776

Our enemies charge us with sedition. In what does it consist? In our refusal to submit to unwarrantable acts of injustice and cruelty? If so, show us a period in your history, in which you have not been equally seditious . . .

> Address to the Inhabitants of Great Britain, by the Continental Congress, 1775

There is a time to preach and a time to fight; and now is the time to fight.

> John Peter Muhlenberg, 1776

The people at large are already sensible that the liberties which America has claimed . . . are not about to fall before the tyranny of foreign conquest; it is native usurpation (of power) that is shaking the foundations of peace.

> Mercy Warren, 1788

Call it independence or what you will, if it is the cause of God and humanity it will go on.

> Tom Paine, 1775

If the great servants of the public forget their duty, betray their trust, and sell their country, or make war against the most valuable rights and privileges of the people, reason and justice require that they should be discarded, and others appointed in their room, without any regard to formal resignations of their forfeited power.

Samuel Langdon, 1775

No republic ever yet stood on a stable foundation without satisfying the common people.

Mercy Warren, 1788

This odious and illegal proclamation must be considered as a plain and full declaration that this despotic viceroy will be bound by no law ... The executing or attempting to execute such proclamation, will justify *resistance* and *reprisal*.

Virginia's instructions to its delegates to the First Continental Congress, 1774

All pretenders to government which have not ultimately the good of the governed in view and do not afford, or endeavor to afford, protection to those over whom they pretend such claims, should, instead of the respects due to legislatures, courts and the like, be esteemed and treated as enemies to society and the rights of mankind.

Ethan Allen, 1780

We do not expect to stand upon any derived power from an arbitrary king; we cannot conceive human nature fallen so low as to be dependent on a crowded head to exist. We expect to stand justified to the world, upon that great principle of reason, that we were created with equal privileges in the scale of human beings, among which is that essential right of making our own laws and choosing our own form of government.

Vermont's Appeal to the World, 1780

Kings and governors may be guilty of treason and rebellion; and they have, in general, in all ages and countries, been more frequently guilty of it than their subjects. Nay, what has been commonly called rebellion in the people has often been nothing else but a glorious struggle in opposition to the lawless power of rebellious kings and princes.

Sam Adams, 1771

VIGILANCE AS THE PRICE OF FREEDOM

There are persons ... who see not the full extent of the evil which threatens them; they solace themselves with hopes that the enemy, if he succeed, will be merciful. It is the madness of folly to expect mercy from those who have refused to do justice; and even mercy, where conquest is the object is only a trick of war; the cunning of the fox is as murderous as the violence of the wolf, and we ought to guard equally against both.

Tom Paine, 1776

Under appearances the most venerable, and institutions the most revered; under the sanctity of religion, the dignity of government, and the smiles of beneficence, do the subtle and ambitious make their first encroachments upon their species. *Watch* and *oppose* ought therefore to be the motto of mankind.

Josiah Quincy, 1774

We must all hang together, or most assuredly, we will all hang separately.

Benjamin Franklin, 1776

'Tis true, that all the mischiefs apprehended by our ancestors from a standing army and excise, have not yet happened. But it does not follow that they will not happen. The inside of a house may catch fire, and the most valuable apartments be ruined, before the flames burst out. The question in these cases is not, what evil has actually attended particular measures—but what evil, in the nature of things, is likely to attend them.

John Dickinson, 1768

Yet, while we rejoice that the adversary has not hitherto prevailed against us, let us by no means put off the harness. Restless malice, and disappointed ambition, will still suggest new measures to our inveterate enemies. Therefore, let us be ready to take the field whenever danger calls; let us be united and strengthen the hands of each other, by promoting a general union among us.

John Hancock, 1774

This is not a season to be mealymouthed, or to mince matters; the times are precarious and perilous.
The Sentinel, 1776

Every man ought to exercise the faculties of his mind, and think and examine for himself, that he may be the less likely to be imposed on, and that he may form as accurate an opinion as possible of the measures of his ruler.

A farmer, 1810

While men could be persuaded they had no rights, or that rights appertained only to a certain class of men, or that government was a thing existing in right of itself, it was not difficult to govern them authoritatively. The ignorance in which they were held, and the superstition in which they were instructed, furnished the means of doing it. But when the ignorance is gone and the superstition with it, when they perceive the imposition that has been acted upon them, and when they reflect that the cultivator and the manufacturer are the primary means of all the wealth that exists in the world beyond what nature spontaneously produces, when they begin to feel their consequences by their usefulness and their right as members of society, it is no longer possible to govern them as before. The fraud, once detected, cannot be retracted. To attempt it is to provoke derision or invite destruction.

Tom Paine, 1776

A spot, a speck of decay, however small the limb on which it appears, and however remote it may seem from the vitals, should be alarming.

John Dickinson, 1768

Let revenge or ambition, pride, lust or profit tempt these men to a base and vile action; you may as well hope to bind up a hungry tiger with a cobweb, as to hold such debauched patriots in the visionary chains of decency, or to charm them with the intellectual beauty of truth and reason.

Abigail Adams, 1775

We have thousands and tens of thousands of anti-revolutionists ready to blow the coals of contention.

William Maclay, 1791

What is become of this spirit, my friends? Is it already, so soon, tired with struggling for your liberties? Or is it altogether evaporated? Not one spark of it left? Are you now contented to let the same set of crafty, dissembling, insinuating men, mere timewatchers, carry their point against you, when you can, with infinitely more ease and safety, counterwork them now more than you could then? I hope not. Only be roused from your sleep; dare to see the Truth, to support the Truth; and the God of Truth will make you free.

Christopher Gadsden, 1769

To reason with despots is throwing reason away. The best of arguments is a vigorous preparation.

Tom Paine, 1792

History affords no example of any nation, country, or people, long free, who did not take some care of themselves; and endeavor to guard and secure their own liberties. Power is of a grasping, encroaching nature . . . Power aims at extending itself, and operating according to mere will, wherever it meets with no balance, check, control, or opposition of any kind. For which reason, it will always be necessary for those who would preserve and perpetuate their liberties to guard them with a wakeful attention.

Jonathan Mayhew, 1766

A bold, ambitious prince, possessed of great abilities, firmly fixed in his throne, served by ministers like himself, and rendered either venerable or terrible by the glory of his successes, may execute what his predecessors did not dare to attempt.

John Dickinson, 1768

If we complain, our complaints are treated with contempt; if we assert our rights, that assertion is deemed insolence; if we humbly offer to submit the matter to the impartial decision of reason, the sword is judged the most proper argument to silence our murmurs! But this cannot long be the case. . .

Joseph Warren, 1772

It is much easier to restrain liberty from running into licentiousness than power from swelling into tyranny and oppression.

Josiah Quincy, 1774

It is the duty of every good citizen to point out what he thinks erroneous in the commonwealth.

James Otis, 1764

No man can be a good member of the community that is not as zealous to oppose tyranny as he is ready to obey magistracy.

Samuel West, 1776

Some persons may think this act of no consequence, because the duties are so *small*. A fatal error. That is the very circumstance most alarming to me. For I am convinced, that the author of this law would never have obtained an act to raise so trifling a sum as it must do, had they not intended by it to establish a precedent for future use.

John Dickinson, 1768

It becomes us to remember that arbitrary power has often originated in justice and necessity.

Benjamin Rush, 1776

Some persons are of the opinion that liberty is not violated, but by such open acts of force; but they seem to be greatly mistaken. Liberty, perhaps, is never exposed to so much danger, as when the people believe there is the least; for it may be subverted and yet they not think so.

John Dickinson, 1768

It is a wise maxim to avoid those things which our enemies wish us to practice.

John Weatherspoon, 1777

As wolves will appear in sheep's clothing, so superlative knaves and parricides will assume the vesture of virtue and patriotism.

Josiah Quincy, 1774

The more elevated the person who errs, the stronger sometimes is the obligation to refute him.

James Otis, 1762

Others, whose minds are unfettered, will think for themselves. They will judge freely of every point of state doctrine and reject with disdain a blind submission to the authority of *mere names*, as being equally ridiculous, as well as dangerous in government and politics.

Sam Adams, 1770

The formalities of a free and the ends of a despotic state have often subsisted together. Thus deceived was the Republic of Rome.

Josiah Quincy, 1774

When I consider, that in every age and country there have been bad men, my heart at this threatening period, is so full of apprehension, as not to permit me to believe, but that there may be some on this continent, against whom you ought to be upon your guard.

John Dickinson, 1768

Let us disappoint the men who are raising themselves on the ruin of this country.

Sam Adams, 1772

MODERATION

A people in love with liberty and sensible to their rights to it . . . ought to be on their guard against unjustifiable and arbitrary claims. Tamely to submit would be highly unworthy of them as free men, and show they deserve the yoke, under which they so readily put their necks.

John Tucker, 1771

When an act injurious to freedom has once been done, and the people bear it, the repetition of it is most likely to meet with submission. For as the mischief of the one was found to be tolerable, they will hope that of the second will prove so too; and they will not regard the infamy of the last, because they are stained with that of the first.

John Dickinson, 1768

It is something of a consolation to be overcome by a lion, but to be devoured by rats is intolerable.

Broadside, signed "Rusticus," 1773

Civil tyranny is usually small in its beginning, like the "drop in the bucket," till at length, like a mighty torrent of raging waves of the sea, it bears down all before it and deluges whole countries and empires ... Tyranny brings ignorance and brutality along with it. It degrades men from their just rank into the class of brutes. It dampens their spirits. It suppresses arts. It extinguishes every spark of noble ardor and generosity in the breasts of those who are enslaved by it. It makes naturally strong and great minds feeble and little and triumphs over the ruins of virtue and humanity. This is true of tyranny in every shape. There can be nothing great and good where its influence reaches. For which reason it becomes every friend to truth and humankind, every lover of God and the Christian religion, to bear a part in opposing this hateful monster ...

Jonathan Mayhew, 1750

Some timid minds are terrified at the word, independence. If you think caution in this respect good
policy, change your mind.

Elbridge Gerry

One of our moderate, prudent friends would be
startled at what I now write. I do not correspond with
such kind of men. You know I never overmuch ad-
mired them. Their moderation has brought us to this
pass; and if they were to be regarded, they would
continue the conflict a century. There are such
moderate men here, but their principles are daily
going out of fashion.

Sam Adams, 1776

Millions entertain no other idea of the legality of
power, then that it is founded on the exercise of
power. They voluntarily fasten their chains, by adopting a pusillanimous opinion "that there will be too
much danger in attempting a remedy."

John Dickinson, 1768

It is presumed no person will publicly, in the pulpit
or otherwise, inculcate the doctrine of passive obedience, or any other doctrine tending to quiet the
minds of the people, in a tame submission to any
unjust imposition.

Town meeting resolution,
New London, Connecticut,
1765

One hundred and seventy-three despots would surely
be as oppressive as one . . . As little will it avail us
that they are chosen by ourselves.

Thomas Jefferson, 1781

If the liberties of America are ever completely ruined
—of which, in my opinion, there is now the utmost
danger—it will in all probability be the consequence
of a mistaken notion of prudence, which leads men to

acquiesce in measures of the most destructive tendency for the sake of present ease. When designs are formed to raze the very foundation of a free government, those few who are to erect their grandeur and fortune upon the general ruin will employ every art to soothe the devoted people into a state of indolence, inattention and security, which is forever the forerunner of slavery. They are alarmed at nothing so much as attempts to awaken the people to *jealousy* and *watchfulness*. And it has been an old game played over and over again, to hold up the men who would rouse their fellow citizens and countrymen to a sense of their *real* danger and spirit them to the most zealous activity in the use of all proper means for preservation of the public liberty, as "pretended patriots", "intemperate politicians", "rash, hotheaded men, incendiaries, wretched desperadoes" who, as was said of the best of men, would turn the world upside-down—or have done it already.

Sam Adams, 1771

A people may be deceived, they may be betrayed by men in whom they put confidence. But they deserve to be abandoned by providence if they trust their interest with men whom they know to be either weak or wicked.

Andrew Elliot, 1765

FIGHTING FOR OUR RIGHTS

Tyranny, like hell, is not easily conquered; yet we have this consolation with us, that the harder the conflict, the more glorious the triumph. What we obtain too cheap, we esteem too lightly; it is dearness only that gives everything its value. Heaven knows how to put a proper price upon its goods; and it would be strange indeed if so celestial an article as FREEDOM should not be highly rated.

Tom Paine, 1776

Trials and conflicts you must, therefore, endure; hazards and jeopardies—of life and fortune—will attend the struggle. Such is the fate of all noble exertions for public liberty and social happiness.

Josiah Quincy, 1774

Men who injure and oppress the people under their administration provoke them to cry out and complain; and then make that very complaint the foundation for new oppressions and prosecutions.

Andrew Hamilton, 1735

The question is not "whether some branches shall be lopped off." The axe is laid to the root of the tree; and the whole body must infallibly perish, if we remain idle spectators of the work.

John Dickinson, 1768

Let no man then suffer his rights to be torn from him for fear of the consequences of defending them—however dreadful they may be, the guilt of them does not lie at his door. If they become arbitrary and use their power against the people who give it, can they suppose that the people in their turn will not use their inherent power against their oppressors, and be as arbitrary as they? When such power is raised, as it is not under the restraint of any regular government or direction, terrible results may generally be expected from it. But those who are answerable for those results are those who raised the tempest.

William Goddard, 1765

Keep up your spirits, and gallantly oppose this adverse course of affairs.

John Dickinson, 1768

I rejoice. I am the first sufferer of liberty since the commencement of our glorious struggle . . . The cause for which I suffer is capable of converting chains into laurels, and transferring a jail into a paradise.

Alexander McDougall, 1770

It is the united voice of America, to preserve their freedom, or lose their lives in defense of it.

Joseph Warren, 1774

Remember that an honorable death is preferable to an ignominious life; and never forget what you owe to yourselves, your families, and your posterity.

Anonymous handbill published
in Philadelphia, 1776

Hath not blood and treasure in all ages been the price of civil liberty? Can the Americans hope a reversal of the laws of our nature, and that the best of blessings will be obtained and secured without the sharpest trials?

Josiah Quincy, 1774

It is now or never, that we must assert our liberty. Twenty years will make the number of tories on this continent equal to the number of patriots. They who shall be born will not have any idea of a free government.

Joseph Hawley, 1774

I expect that many will adore the rising sun; they will fawn and flatter and even lick the dust of their master's feet. But you and I acknowledge no master. It is no dishonor to be in a minority in the cause of liberty and virtue.

Sam Adams, 1771

Ye dark designing knaves, ye murderers, parricides! How dare you tread upon the earth, which has drunk in the blood of slaughtered innocents, shed by your wicked hands?

> John Hancock (on the anniversary of the Boston Massacre), 1774

Whoever considers the unprincipled enemy we have to cope with, will not hesitate to declare that nothing but arms or miracles can reduce them to reason and moderation. They have lost sight of the limits of humanity. Our enemies have mistaken our peace for cowardice, and supposing us unarmed have begun the attack.

> Tom Paine, 1775

What has commonly been called rebellion has more often been nothing but a glorious struggle in opposition to the lawless power of rebellious kings and princes. If ye love wealth better than liberty, the tranquility of servitude better than the animating contest of freedom, go home from us in peace. We ask not your counsels or arms. Crouch down and lick the hands which feed you. May your chains set lightly upon you, and may posterity forget that you were our countrymen.

> Sam Adams, 1776

Mr. Strahan—You are a member of Parliament, and one of that majority which has doomed my country to destruction. You have begun to burn our towns and murder our people. Look upon your hands; they are stained with the blood of your relations! You and I were long friends; you are now my enemy, and I am, Yours,

> Benjamin Franklin, 1775

I would tell (the government) that we had borne much, that the spirit of freedom beats too high in us to submit to slavery, and that, if nothing else would satisfy a tyrant and his diabolical ministry, we are determined to shake off all connections with a state so unjust and unnatural. This I would tell them, not under cover, but in words as clear as the sun in its meridian brightness.

George Washington, 1776

Some there are, who acknowledging, for who can deny it, the violation of our liberties, yet think there is a necessity of submitting to it. But, for my part, I cannot conceive the necessity of becoming a slave, while there remains a ditch in which one may die free!

Arthur Lee, 1768

Sir—You will hear from us with astonishment. You ought to hear from us with horror. You are charge-able before God and man, with our blood. The soldiers are but passive instruments ... You were a free agent. You acted coolly, deliberately and with all that premeditated malice, not against us in par-ticular but the people in general, which, in the sight of the law is an ingredient in the composition of murder. You will hear further from us.

John Adams (quoting a speech by Crispus Attucks), 1773

They still talk big in England and threaten hard; but their language is somewhat civiler, at least not quite so disrespectful to us. By degrees, they come to their senses, but too late, I fancy, for their interest. There is a kind of suspense in men's minds here at present, waiting to see what terms will be offered. I expect none that we can accept; and when that is generally seen, we shall be more unanimous and more decisive.

Benjamin Franklin, 1776

DIVIDE AND TYRANNIZE. Would to heaven that I could hang a comet on every letter of this motto, to warn my countrymen of the danger that threatens their liberties from the adoption of this maxim into the (government) counsels respecting America. Let us manifest to all the world, how unanimously we are determined, both with hand and heart, to maintain our freedom and frustrate the designs of those, who, by dividing would enslave us.

Arthur Lee, 1768

If you're men, behave like men. Let's take up arms immediately, and be free, and seize all the King's officers.

Sam Adams

No character appears with a stronger luster in my mind than that of a man who nobly perseveres in the cause of public liberty and virtue, through the rage of persecution. Of this, you have had a large portion, but I dare say you are made the better by it. At least I will venture to say that the sharpest persecution for the sake of one's country can never prove a real injury to an honest man. In this little part of the world—a land till of late happy in its obscurity—the asylum to which patriots were formerly wont to make their peaceful retreat; even here the stern tyrant has lifted up his iron rod and makes his incessant claim as *lord of the soil*. But I have a firm persuasion in my mind that, in every struggle, this country will prove herself as glorious in defending and maintaining her freedom as she has heretofore been happy in enjoying it.

Sam Adams (to John Wilkes, the imprisoned English radical), 1770

I find everywhere some men, who are afraid of a free government, lest it should be perverted and made use of as a cloak for licenciousness. The fear of the peoples abusing their liberty is made an argument against their having the enjoyment of it; as if anything were so much to be dreaded by mankind as slavery.

Sam Adams, 1775

The feelings of the heart will dictate the language of truth, and the simplicity of her assets will proclaim the infamy of those who betray the rights of the people under the pretense of *justice, consolidation,* and *dignity.*

Mercy Warren, 1788

THE GOVERNMENT

THE EXECUTIVE BRANCH AND GOVERNMENT BUREAUCRACY

In every stage of these oppressions we have petitioned for redress in the most humble terms: Our repeated petitions have been answered only by repeated injury. A prince whose character is thus marked by every act which may define a tyrant, is unfit to be the ruler of a free people.

The Declaration of Independence, 1776

I will not say that our King hath committed willful and corrupt perjury . . . neither do I assert that the people are now absolved from their allegiance; but . . . *nobody can be hanged for thinking.*

Virginia Gazette, 1774

(The King) is no more than the chief officer of the people, appointed by laws, and circumscribed with definite powers, to assist in working the great machine of government erected for their use and consequently, subject to their superintendence.

Thomas Jefferson, 1774

(We lay our grievances before you) with that freedom of language and sentiment which becomes a free people claiming their rights, as derived from the laws of nature and not as the gift of their chief magistrate. Let those flatter who fear: it is not an American art. To give praise which is not due might well be from the venal, but would ill beseem those who are asserting the rights of human nature. They know, and will therefore say ... that kings are the servants, not the proprietors, of the people. Open your breast, sire, to liberal and expanded thought. Let not the name of George III be a blot on the page of history . . . The great principles of right and wrong are legible to every reader; to pursue them requires not the aid of many counsellors. The whole art of government consists in the art of being honest. Only aim to do your duty and mankind will give you credit where you fail . . .

Thomas Jefferson (to George III), 1774

Although (kings) are beings of our own creating, they know us not, and are become the gods of their creators.

Tom Paine, *Common Sense*, 1776

Shall we hope a minister so wicked and so daring will never live? Vain hope, even now he lives.

Arthur Lee, 1768

You may use your proclamations, and welcome, for we have learned to reverence ourselves and scorn the insulting ruffian that employs you.

Tom Paine, *The Crisis*, No. 2, 1777

To the persecution and tyranny of his cruel ministry we will not tamely submit—appealing to Heaven for the justice of our cause, we determine to die or be free.

> Joseph Warren, Address to the
> Massachusetts Provincial
> Congress, 1775

Gods! Are we men, and shall we suffer the foundation to be laid for miseries like these; shall we look tamely on while the yoke is fixed upon us, under which we must forever groan? We and our posterity forever. Shall we thus devote ourselves and them to be hunted like beasts of prey, like murderers and felons; our property, our liberty, our happiness given up to ministers, who having grown savage in the exercise of despotism, shall contrive for us new hardships, new oppressions, and tyrannize without measure, without fear, without mercy?

> Arthur Lee, 1768

If rulers are a terror to good works and not to the evil; if they are not ministers for good to society but for evil and distress by violence and oppression; if they execute wrath upon sober, peaceable persons who do their duty as members of society, and suffer rich and honorable knaves to escape with impunity; if, instead of continually advancing the public welfare, they attend only upon the gratification of their own lust and pride and ambition to the destruction of public welfare—if this be the case, it is plain that the Apostle's argument for submission does not reach them . . . Rulers have no authority from God to do mischief . . . Laws tempered and accommodated to the common welfare of the subjects must be supposed to be agreeable to the will of the beneficent Author and supreme Lord of the universe whose kingdom ruleth over all and whose tender mercies are over all his works. It is blasphemy to call tyrants and oppressors God's ministers but such as are just, ruling in the fear of God. When once magistrates act contrary to their office and the end of their institution, when they rob and ruin the public instead of being guardians of its peace and welfare, they immediately cease to be the ordinance and ministers of God and no more deserve that glorious character than common pirates and highwaymen.

> Jonathan Mayhew, *A discourse concerning unlimited submission and non-resistance to higher powers*, 1750

He has erected a multitude of new offices, and sent hither swarms of officers to harass our people, and eat out their substance.

> The Declaration of Independence, 1776

The time, sir, will come when you, in a melancholy hour, shall reckon up your miseries by your murders in America.

> Thomas Paine, *The Crisis*, No. 5 (Addressed to Lord Howe), 1778

Nothing can well be imagined more directly contrary to common sense than to suppose that millions of people should be subjected to the arbitrary, precarious pleasure of a single man.

> Jonathan Mayhew, 1756

Many things which appear of little importance at the beginning may have great durable consequences from their having been established at the commencement of a new ... government. It will be much easier to commence the administration, upon a well adjusted system, built on tenable grounds, than to correct errors or alter inconveniences after they shall have been confirmed by habit.

> George Washington

The executive may refuse its assent to necessary measures till new appointments shall be referred to him. And having by degrees exposed all these into his own hands, the American Executive, like the British, will by bribery and influence, save himself the trouble and odium of exerting his negative afterwards. We are, Mr. Chairman, going very far in this business. We are not indeed constituting a British Government, but a more dangerous monarchy—an elective one!

George Mason, 1787

No point is of more importance than that the right of impeachment should be continued. Shall any man be above justice? Above all, should that man be above it who can commit the most injustice?

George Mason, 1787

This royal, arbitrary line in the time of kingly power was, in the nature of it, incompatible with the rights of a free people, as they were thereby divested of the inestimable privilege of choosing their own form of government and of electing their own magistrates; nor were they in such circumstances in any condition to know what form or alteration of government might next take place, as the king and his creatures were the sole arbitrators of it.

Ethan Allen, 1772

There is nothing more becoming to human nature than well ordered government, or more valuable than liberty. How ignominious then must his conduct be who turns the first into confusion, and the latter into slavery.

William Rind, 1769

Guilt wherever found should be punished. The executive will have great opportunities of abusing his power —particularly in time of war, when the military force and in some respects the public money will be in his hands.

Edmund Randolph

The spirit of encroachment tends to consolidate the powers of all the departments in one, and thus to create, whatever the form of government, a real despotism.

George Washington, 1796

The second grade or stage is to create and multiply officers and appointments under the general government by every possible means in the diplomacy, judiciary and military. This is called giving the President a respectable patronage—a term, I confess, new to me in the present sense of it, which I take to mean neither more nor less than that the President should always have a number of places in his gift to reward those members of Congress who may promote his views or support his measures; more especially if by such conduct they should forfeit the esteem of their constituents. We talk of corruption in Great Britain. I pray we may not have occasion for complaints of a similar nature here.

William Maclay, 1790

The first magistrate of a country . . . seldom knows the real state of the nation, particularly if he be buoyed up by official importance to think it is beneath his dignity to mix occasionally with the people.

Philip Freneau

When society has deputed a certain number of their equals to take care of their personal rights and the interest of the whole community, it must be considered that responsibility is the great security of integrity and honour.

Mercy Warren, 1788

Can you think that this country is to be finally subdued by a man who never possessed real greatness, and with all his art could never counterfeit it?

Sam Adams, 1771

Caesar had his Brutus, Charles the First his Cromwell, and George the Third may profit by their example . . .

> Patrick Henry, 1765

Political power in one man, without division or responsibility, is monarchy. The same power in a few is aristocracy. And the same power in the whole nation is democracy. And the resemblance of our system of government to either of these forms depends upon the resemblance of a president or a governor to a monarch, or an American Senate to an hereditary order, and of a house of representatives to a legislating nation.

> John Taylor, 1814

Be assured, sir, no occurrence in the course of the war has given me more painful sensations than your information of there being such ideas existing in the army . . . I am much at a loss to conceive what part of my conduct could have given encouragement to an address which to me seems big with the greatest mischiefs that can befall my country. If I am not deceived in the knowledge of myself, you could not have found a person to whom your schemes are more disagreeable.

> George Washington (replying to a suggestion that he become king), 1782

History furnishes one example only of a first magistrate being brought to public justice. Everybody cried out against this as unconstitutional. What was practice before in cases where the chief magistrate rendered himself obnoxious? Why, recourse was had to assassination in which he was not only deprived of his life, but of the opportunity of vindicating his character. It would be the best way, therefore, to provide in the Constitution for the regular punishment of the executive when his misconduct would deserve it, and for his honorable acquittal when he should be unjustly accused.

Benjamin Franklin

Government is instituted for the protection, safety, and happiness of the people, and not for the profit, honour, or private interest of any man, family, or class of men.

Mercy Warren, 1788

POLITICIANS

The people plainly see that a change of men is not likely to produce a change of measures—so soon are the words of the one verified, when he said of the other that he could rely upon him as he could rely upon himself.

Sam Adams, 1770

The smaller the society, the fewer probably will be the distinct parties and interests composing it; the fewer the distinct parties and interests the more frequently will a majority be found of the same party, and the smaller the compass within which they are placed, the more easily will they concert and execute their plans of oppression.

James Madison

In every corner ambitious men abound, for ignorance or want of qualifications is no bar to this view ... The government (may) be bandied about from one set of projectors to another, till some one man more artful than the rest, to perpetuate their power, slip the noose of despotism about our necks. Tis easy to say this never can happen among a virtuous people— Ay, but we are not more virtuous than the nations which have gone before us.

William Maclay, 1791

Were we chosen with dictatorial powers, or were we sent forward as servants of the public, to do their business? The latter, clearly.

William Maclay, 1791

To cure distemper of old governments is an infinitely arduous task, to erect a new on wise and lasting principles is the greatest task the mind of man can undertake. Those who are employed in the execution of it besides an uncorruptable virtue ought to be endowed with the most extraordinary gifts of nature, accompanied by a comprehensive knowledge of history and of mankind. They ought to be well versed in all the governments of ancient and modern states; to be well acquainted with the revolutions that have happened in them, the causes and the effects.

The Sentinel, 1776

If once the people become inattentive to the public affairs you and I and Congress and assemblies, judges and governors, shall all become wolves. It seems to be the law of our general nature, in spite of individual exceptions.

Thomas Jefferson, 1787

I am not a Federalist, because I never submitted the whole system of my opinions to the creed of any party of men whatever in religion, in philosophy, in politics, or in any thing else where I was capable of thinking for myself. Such an addition is the last degradation of a free and moral agent. If I could not go to heaven but with a party, I would not go there at all.

Thomas Jefferson, 1789

I am no party man, unless a firm attachment to the cause of liberty and truth will denominate one such. And if this be the judgement of those who have taken upon themselves the character of *friends to the government*, I am content to be in their sense of the word, a party man, and will glory in it as long as I shall retain that small portion of understanding which God has been pleased to bless me with.

Sam Adams, 1771

I recommend it to my sons, from my own experience in life, to prefer the happiness of independence and a private station to the troubles and vexation of public business: but if either their own inclinations or the necessity of the times should engage them in public affairs, I charge them on a father's blessing, never to let the motives of private interest or ambition induce them to betray, nor the terrors of poverty and disgrace, or the fear of danger or of death, deter them from asserting the liberty of their country, and endeavoring to transmit to their posterity those sacred rights to which they themselves were born.

George Mason (last will and testament)

Whenever those bounds are exceeded, the people have a right to reassume the exercise of that authority which by nature they had before they delegated it to individuals.

Town meeting of New London, Connecticut, 1765

The long duration of Parliment is allowed by all to be the principal cause of its present corrupt state. The members, by being so long in power forget their dependence on the people, and the ministry, knowing they are to continue for seven years, think it worth their while to seduce them with a high bribe. If they were elected annually or even triannually, they would feel themselves more dependent upon their constituents and would take greater pains to please them.

The ministry could not afford in that case to offer a bribe high enough to corrupt their honesty or make it in their interest to fell and betray their constituents; political quacks are the most dangerous of all men if they have influence.

The Sentinel, 1776

ABUSE AND USURPATION OF POWER

Sanctified by authority and armed with power, error and usurpation bid defiance to truth and right . . .
Josiah Quincy, 1774

But it cannot be supposed that a community will be so attentive but upon the most alarming events. In general, individuals are following their private concerns, while it is to be feared the restless adversaries are forming the most dangerous plans for the ruin of the reputation of the people, in order to build their own greatness on the destruction of their liberties . . . Such a conduct, if allowed, seems to put it into the power of a combination of a few designing men to deceive a nation to its ruin.

The Boston Committee (to
Benjamin Franklin), 1770

As great a blessing as government is, like other blessings, it may become a scourge, a curse, and severe punishment to a people.

Reverend Peter Whitney, 1774

A lust of domination is more or less natural to all parties; and hence the stupidity of entrusting any set of people with more power than necessity requires. Ambition and a thirst for sway are so deeply implanted in the human mind that one degree of elevation serves only as a step by which to ascend the next; nor can they ever mount the ladder so high as not to find the top still equally remote.

The New York Mercury, 1755

Single acts of tyranny may be ascribed to the accidental opinion of a day; but a series of oppressions, begun at a distinguished period and pursued unalterably through every change of ministers, too plainly proves a deliberate, systematical plan of reducing us to slavery.

Thomas Jefferson, 1774

I have ever been a friend to the Federal Government; but I never meant to dupe others and hope I shall not be duped myself. I remember well that when the Constitution was disputed about, every one declared that the powers therein granted, were so particularly enumerated that no powers, not meant to be granted, could ever be pretended to, and that the line between them and the state powers was so clearly drawn that these could never be broken in upon—I have always supposed and have often said this myself. But now a new doctrine is set up and we are told we are not to look for the rule of Congress in these particular powers inasmuch as they can make laws in all cases whatever, where, in their discretion and by possibility the laws will promote the general welfare, and the subject of them will admit of money being applied. Is not this saying in a roundabout way, but in very plain terms, that Congress may do what they please? For they may give the name of 'general welfare' to anything, and by possibility any thing almost may operate generally, and as to the application of money, we all know that scarce anything can be done without it, and that it is much easier for any government to apply it than for the people to pay it.

The Federal Gazette, 1792

These were no longer the votes then of the representatives of the people, but of deserters from the rights and interests of the people; and it was impossible to consider their decisions, which had nothing in view but to enrich themselves, as the measure of the fair majority, which ought always to be respected.

Thomas Jefferson

Monarchy is a government fit only for a people whose vices the fear of punishment alone is able to restrain.

Mercy Warren, 1788

Nothing can be more aggravated than for the shepherds to mislead and butcher the flock they were set to defend and feed! And the guardians of the public interests, to turn traitors and assassins to them that raised them to their high places.

Samuel Webster, 1777

Perhaps there never was a time when the political affairs of America were in a more dangerous state. Those who are the appointed instruments of oppression have all the means put into their hands of applying to the passions of men and availing themselves of the necessities of some, the vanity of others and the timidity of all.

Sam Adams, 1771

Such is the complacency these great men have for the smiles of their prince that they will gratify every desire of ambition and power at the expense of truth, reason, and their country.

John Dickinson, 1768

Experience has shown that even under the best forms (of government) those entrusted with power have, in time, and by slow operations perverted it into tyranny.

Thomas Jefferson, 1779

Unlimited power has generally been destructive of human happiness. The people are not under such temptations to thwart their own interests, as absolute government is under to abuse the people.

Charles Turner, 1773

Monarchy is a species of government fit only for a people too much corrupted by luxury, avarice and a passion for pleasure to have any love for their country.

Mercy Warren, 1788

... the people may apprehend that they have just reason to complain of oppression and wrong, and to be jealous of their liberties, when subordinate public offices are made the surest step to wealth and ease.

Samuel Cooke, 1770

When kings, ministers, governors, or legislators, therefore, instead of exercising the powers entrusted with them according to the principles, forms, and proportions stated by the constitution and established by the original compact, prostitute those powers to the purposes of oppression—to subvert instead of supporting, a free constitution—to destroy instead of preserving the lives, liberties, and properties of the people—they are no longer to be deemed magistrates vested with a sacred character, but become public enemies and ought to be resisted!

Proclamation of the General
Court of Massachusetts, 1776

The ministry must go out, and give place to men of juster and more generous principles. If you divide, you are lost.

Benjamin Franklin, 1774

The just ruler will not fear to have his public conduct critically inspected, but will choose to recommend himself to the approbation of every man.

Samuel Cooke, 1770

A prince, whose character is thus marked by every act which may define a tyrant, is unfit to be the ruler of a free people.

> The Declaration of Independence, 1776

We are reduced to the alternative of choosing between an unconditional submission to the tyranny of irritated ministers, or resistance by force. The latter is our choice . . . We have counted the cost of this contest, and find nothing so dreadful as voluntary slavery . . . Our cause is just . . . the arms we have been compelled by our enemies to assume, we will, in defiance of every hazard, with unabating firmness and perseverance, employ for the preservation of our liberties; being with one mind resolved to die freemen rather than live slaves.

> Declaration of Causes on Taking up Arms, Continental Congress, 1775

CORRUPTION

Power is intoxicating. There have been few men, if any, who when possessed of an unrestrained power, have not made a very bad use of it.

> Sam Adams, 1771

There is something in corruption, which, like a jaundiced eye, transfers the color of itself to the object it looks upon, and sees everything stained and impure.

> Tom Paine, *The Crisis*, No. 6, 1778

A system is daily developing itself which must gradually undermine and destroy our so much boasted equality, liberty and republicanism—high wages, ample compensations, great salaries to every person connected with the government of the United States.
William Maclay, 1790

Do you behold an exclusive mass of virtue, almost inducing you to exclaim: *These are the sons of the Gods*? Do you behold an exclusive mass of talents, compelling you to acknowledge that these are sages qualified to govern? . . . Truth compels you to acknowledge that you cannot discern a solitary particle of these qualities so essential to aristocracy.
John Taylor, *Inquiry*, 1814

Is it not conceivable that a political system founded in good moral principles is discoverable, capable of dispensing good, independently of the vices of its administrators?
John Taylor, 1814

One who entered this contest from a pure love of liberty and a sense of injured rights, who determined to make every sacrifice . . . to place the powers of governing him in a plurality of hands of his own choice, so that the corrupt will of no one man might in future oppress him, must stand confounded and dismayed when he is told that a considerable portion of that plurality has mediated the surrender of them into a single hand, and, in lieu of a limited monarchy, to deliver him over to a despotic one! How must he find his efforts and sacrifices abused and baffled, if he may still, by a single vote, be laid prostrate at the feet of one man! In God's name—from whence have they derived this power? Is it from our ancient laws? None such can be produced. Is it from any principle in our new Constitution, expressed or implied? Every lineament expressed or implied is in full opposition to it! . . . Our ancient laws expressly declare that those who are but delegates themselves shall not delegate to others powers which require judgment and integrity in their exercise. Or was this proposition moved on a supposed right in the movers of abandoning their posts in a moment of distress? The same laws forbid the abandonment of that post, even on ordinary occasions; and much more a transfer of their powers into other hands and other forms, without consulting the people!

Thomas Jefferson, *Notes on Virginia*, 1782

The influence of wealth at elections is irresistible,
Benjamin Rush, 1777

When once magistrates act contrary to their office and the end of their institution, when they rob and ruin the public instead of being guardians of its peace and welfare, they immediately cease to be the ordinance and ministers of God and no more deserve that glorious character than common pirates and highwaymen.

Jonathan Mayhew, 1750

Such a legislature will create unnecessary offices that themselves or their relations may be endowed with them. They will lavish the revenue to enrich themselves. They will borrow for the nation that they may lend. They will offer lenders great profits that they may share in them. As grievances gradually excite national discontent, they will fix the yoke more securely by making it gradually heavier. And they will finally avow and maintain their corruption by establishing an irresistible standing army, not to defend the nation but to defend a system for plundering the nation.

John Taylor, *Inquiry*, 1814

Rulers have no authority from God to do mischief . . .
Jonathan Mayhew, 1750

The King never had in the province so vile a set of
servants in the Custom House as there are present—
not moved by any considerations except such as tend
immediately to their interests.

Henry Laurens, 1769

Is there any man whose public conduct will not bear
the scrutiny of truth? He is a traitor, and it is high
time he was pointed out.

Sam Adams, 1771

Absolute power should never be trusted to man. It
has perverted the wisest heads, and corrupted the
best hearts in the world.

Benjamin Rush, 1777

Corruption and freedom cannot long subsist together.

Charles Carroll, Sr., 1763

Government was instituted for the purposes of common defense; and those who hold the reins of government have an equitable natural right to an honorable
support from the same principle—'that the laborer
is worthy of his hire.'

Sam Adams, 1772

We have too many high sounding words, and too
few actions that correspond with them.

Abigail Adams, 1774

Aristocracy is.a still more formidable foe to public
virtue; under such a government her patriots become
mercenaries, her soldiers cowards, and the people
slaves.

Mercy Warren, 1788

ECONOMICS

ECONOMIC TYRANNY

The poverty of the country is such that all the power and sway has got into the hands of the rich, who by extortious advantages, having the common people in their debt, have always curbed and oppressed them in all manner of ways.

Nathaniel Bacon, 1676

Where wealth is hereditary, power is hereditary; for wealth is power. Titles are of very little or of no consequence. The rich are nobility, and the poor plebians in all countries. And on this distinction alone the true definition of aristocracy depends. And aristocracy is that influence or power which property may have in government; a democracy is the power or influence of the people or members, as contra-distinguished from property. Between these two

146

powers—the aristocracy and democracy—that is, the rich and the poor, there is constant warfare.

A farmer in the *Maryland Gazette*, 1783

Wealth tends to corrupt the mind and to nourish its love of power, and to stimulate it to oppression.

Gouveneur Morris

Superfluous property is the creature of society. Simple and mild laws were sufficient to guard the property that was merely necessary. When, by virtue of the first laws, part of the society accumulated wealth and grew powerful, they enacted others more severe, and would protect their property to the expense of humanity. This was abusing their power and commencing a tyranny.

Benjamin Franklin, 1785

Aristocracy has abandoned a reliance on a monopoly of virtue, reknown or abilities, and resorted wholly to a monopoly of wealth.

John Taylor, 1814

A people is travelling fast to destruction, when individuals consider their interests as distinct from those of the public. Such notions are fatal to their country and to themselves. Yet how many there are, so weak and sordid as to think they perform all the offices of life, if they earnestly endeavour to increase their own wealth, power and credit without the least regard for the society, under the protection of which they live; who, if they can make an immediate profit to themselves, by lending their assistance to those whose projects plainly tend to the injury of their country, rejoice in dexterity, and believe themselves entitled to the character of able politicians. Miserable men! Of whom it is hard to say whether they ought to be most the objects of pity or contempt. But whose opinions are certainly as detestable as their practices are destructive.

John Dickinson, 1768

The most common and durable source of faction has been the various and unequal distribution of property.

James Madison, *The Federalist*, No. 10

Experience declares that man is the only animal which devours his own kind, for I can apply no milder term . . . to the general prey of the rich on the poor.

Thomas Jefferson, 1787

What is the history of mighty kingdoms and nations, but a detail of the ravages and cruelties of the powerful over the weak?

Abigail Adams, 1783

The contrast of affluence and wretchedness continually meeting and offending the eye, is like dead and living bodies chained together.

Tom Paine, 1796

That some desperate wretches should be willing to steal and enslave men by violence and murder for gain, is rather lamentable than strange.

Tom Paine, 1775

I have lately made a tour through Ireland and Scotland. In those countries a small part of the society are Landlords, great noblemen, and gentlemen, extremely opulent, living in the highest affluence and magnificence: the bulk of the people tenants, extremely poor, living in the most sordid wretchedness, in dirty hovels of mud and straw, and cloathed only in rags . . . in the possession and enjoyment of the various comforts of life, compared to these people every Indian is a gentleman; And the effect of this kind of civil society seems to be, depressing the multitudes below the savage state that a few may be raised above it.

Benjamin Franklin, 1772

ATTENTION!—to the British Commissaries, British insinuations, and British arts, take care that their *gold* be not more fatal to you than their *lead*. The last has slain its thousands, the first may purchase chains for millions. Observe where it is like to go; mark its effect in every order; and let the sovereign remedy be ever kept, a wakeful attention in the body of the people.

"Bob Centinel," *New York Journal*, 1778

Those who have once got an ascendancy and possessed themselves of all the resources of the nations . . . have immense means for retaining their advantage.

Thomas Jefferson

All hereditary government is in its nature tyranny. An hereditable or unhereditable throne, or by what other fanciful name such things may be called, have no other significant explanation than that mankind are hereditable property. To inherit the government is to inherit the people, as if they were flocks and herds.

Tom Paine, *The Rights of Man*, 1792

Civilization . . . has operated two ways, to make one part of society more affluent and the other part more wretched than would have been the lot of either in a natural state.

Tom Paine, 1796

The accumulation of personal property is, in many instances, the effect of paying too little for the labor that produced it, the consequence of which is, that the working hand perishes in old age, and the employer abounds in affluence.

Tom Paine, 1795

No free people ever existed, or can exist, without keeping "the purse strings" in their own hands.

Where this is a case, they have a constitutional check upon the administration, which may thereby be brought into order without violence. But where such a power is not lodged in the *people*, oppression proceeds uncontrolled in its career, till the governed, transported into rage, seek redress in the midst of blood and confusion.

John Dickinson, 1768

ECONOMIC DEMOCRACY

To enjoy the fruits of our own honest industry; to call that our own which we earn with the labor of our hands, and the sweat of our brows; to regulate that internal policy by which we, and not they, are to be affected; these are the mighty boons we ask. And traitors, rebels and every harsh appellation that malice can dictate, or the violence of language express, are the returns which we receive to the most humble petitions and earnest supplications.

Proclamation of the State of
North Carolina, 1775

In what does real power consist? The answer is short and plain—in property. A general and tolerably equal distribution of landed property is the whole basis of national freedom.

Noah Webster, *An Examination
into the Leading Principles of
the Federal Constitution Proposed by the Late Convention
held at Philadelphia*, 1787

The protection of a man's person is more sacred than the protection of property; and besides this, the faculty of performing any kind of work or services by which he acquires a livelihood or maintains a family is of the nature of property. It is property in him.

> Tom Paine, *The Rights of Man*, 1792

Let these truths be indelibly impressed on our minds—*That we cannot be happy without being free*—that we cannot be free *without being secure in our property*—that we cannot be secure in our property if, without our consent, others may, as by right, take it away—that duties laid for the sole purpose of raising money are taxes—that attempts to lay such duties should be instantly and firmly opposed.

> *The New York Journal*, 1768

An equality of property, with a necessity of alienation constantly operating to destroy combinations of powerful families, is the very soul of a republic. While this continues, the people will inevitably possess both power and freedom; when this is lost, power departs, liberty expires, and a commonwealth will inevitably assume some other form.

> Noah Webster, 1787

In every society where property exists there will ever be a struggle between rich and poor. Mixed in one assembly, equal laws can never be expected.

> John Adams

No hereditary emoluments, privileges or honors ought to be granted or conferred in this State . . . Perpetuities and monopolies are contrary to the genius of a free state and ought not be allowed.

> Section 22, North Carolina
> Declaration of Rights, 1776

Blessed by God, there is sufficiency in the land of the necessities of life; and if somebody is not wanting, all the poor may be supplied. And as, to many, if not most, foreign articles, there is undoubtedly a considerable supply. How then comes it to pass that such mutual jealousies should arise, as to make an artificial scarcity where we all know there is none? For God's sake, don't let us counterfeit a scarcity lest He bring a real one! But let town and country open their stores and their hands, and, to the utmost of their power, supply each other.

Samuel Webster, 1777

Industry and constant employment are great preservations of the morals and virtue of a nation.

Benjamin Franklin

Wealth gotten by vanity shall be diminished, but he that gathereth by labour shall increase.

Simon Peter, *The Federal Gazette*, 1792

Private property is a creature of society, and is subject to the calls of that society, whenever its necessities shall require it, even to its last farthing.

Benjamin Franklin, 1783

Alienation (of land) is the remedy for an aristocracy founded on landed wealth, inhibitions upon monopoly and incorporation for one founded upon paper wealth.

John Taylor, *Inquiry*, 1814

I care not how affluent some may be provided that none be miserable in consequence of it.

Tom Paine, 1796

Then might perhaps one land on earth be found,
Free from the extremes of poverty and riches,

Where ne'er a sceptered tyrant should be known,
Or tyrant lordling, curses of creation?

> "Seward" in William Dunlap's
> play *The Father*, 1789

Deeply impressed with a sense of our duty to our country, paternal affection for our children and un-born millions, as also for our personal rights and liberties, we solemnly convenant that we will not do or perform any blacksmith's work or business of any kind, for any person or persons commonly known by the name of Tories."

> Blacksmith's convention of
> Worcester County,
> Massachusetts, 1774

At these meetings the lowest mechanics discuss upon the most important points of government, with the utmost freedom.

> Tory description of town meetings, 1768

BANKS AND CORPORATIONS

I sincerely believe, with you, that banking establish-ments are more dangerous than standing armies.

> Thomas Jefferson, 1816

I have no great predilection for banks. They may be considered, in some measure, as operating like a tax in favor of the rich, against the poor; tending to the accumulating in a few hands; and yet stock, wealth, money or property of any kind whatever accumulated, has a similar effect.

William Maclay, 1790

I do not know whether you may recollect how loudly my voice was raised against the establishment of banks in the beginning; but like that of Cassandra it was not listened to. I was set down as a madman by those who have since been victims to them.

Thomas Jefferson, 1823

The rapid and exorbitant rise upon the necessaries and conveniences of life . . . is chiefly occasioned by monopolizers, that great pest of society, who prefer their own private gain to the interest and safety of their country.

Connecticut price-fixing legislation, 1776

I hope we shall crush in its birth the aristocracy of our moneyed corporations, which dare already to challenge our government to a trial of strength and bid defiance to the laws of our country.

Thomas Jefferson, 1814

(Monopolies are) odious, contrary to the principles of a free government, and the principles of commerce.

Maryland revolutionary constitution, 1776

(The corporation) penetrating its every part of the Union, acting by command and in phalanx, may, in a critical moment, upset the government. I deem no government safe which is under the vassalage of any self-constituted authorities.

Thomas Jefferson

Let monopolies and all kinds and degrees of oppression be carefully guarded against.
> Samuel Webster, 1777

The dominion of the banks must be broken, or it will break us.
> Thomas Jefferson, 1815

Have not our funding system and its offspring, banks, like so many Delilahs robbed the whigs of their revolutionary strength and virtue? War has its evils; so has a long peace. A field of battle covered with dead bodies putrefying in the open air is an awful and distressing spectacle, but a nation debased by the love of money and exhibiting all the vices and crimes usually connected with that passion, is a spectacle far more awful, distressing and offensive.
> Benjamin Rush to Thomas Jefferson, 1813

Everything predicted by the enemies of banks in the beginning, is now coming to pass.
> Thomas Jefferson, 1814

I was much struck with your strictures upon banks. They have long governed all our state legislatures. A few weeks will determine whether the general government has strength enough to resist the power of one of them. Is there any difference in point of criminality between bribing public bodies and individuals? The funding system was carried by bribing both.
> Benjamin Rush, 1811

Creditors have better memories than debtors.
> Benjamin Franklin, *Poor Richard's Almanac*, 1758

I did not think politics would have reached this retreat I have chosen; but you have called on me for my sentiments, and when our country is in danger, no man ought excuse himself. I have trespassed too long on your patience. I shall therefore conclude with a proposal that your watchmen be instructed, as they go on their rounds, to call out every night, half-past twelve, beware of the East India Company.

Broadside, signed "Rusticus," 1773

It is said that paper systems, being open to all, are not monopolies. He who has money may buy stock. All then is fair, as every man (meaning, however, only every monied man) may share in the plunder. (Well), every man may enlist in an army, yet an army may enslave a nation.

John Taylor, 1814

TAXES

Arbitrary taxation is plunder authorized by law: it is the support and the essence of tyranny, and has done more mischief to mankind than the other three scourges from Heaven—famine, pestilence and the sword.

The Maryland Gazette, 1774

Modern taxes and frauds to collect money . . . afford the best evidence of the present character of aristocracy.

John Taylor, 1814

They may lay a poll tax. This is simple and easily collected, but it is of all taxes the most grievous. Why the most grievous? Because it falls light on the rich and heavy on the poor. It is most oppressive, for if the rich man is taxed, he can only retrench his superfluities; but the consequence to the poor man is that it increases his miseries.

George Mason, 1788

Considering the general tendency to multiply offices and dependencies, and to increase expense to the ultimate term of burden which citizens can bear, it behooves us to avail ourselves of every occasion which presents itself for taking off the surcharge; That it may never be seen here that, after leaving to labor the smallest portion of its earnings on which it can subsist, government itself shall consume the residue of what it was instituted to guard.

Thomas Jefferson, *First Annual Message*, 1801

If taxes are laid upon us without our having a legal representation where they are laid, we are reduced from the character of free subjects to the state of tributary slaves.

Sam Adams, 1764

The purchaser of any article, very seldom reflects that the seller raises his prices, so as to indemnify himself for the tax *he* has paid. He knows that the prices of things are continually fluctuating, and if he thinks about the tax, he thinks at the same time, that he *might* have paid as much, if the article he buys had not been taxed. He gets something visible and agreeable for his money; and tax and price are so confounded together, that he cannot separate, or does not choose to take the trouble of separating them. This mode of taxation therefore is the most suited to arbitrary and oppressive governments.

John Dickinson, 1768

Be taxed, or not be taxed; that is the question.
Whether 'tis nobler in our minds to suffer
The flights and cunning of deceitful statesmen,
Or to petition 'gainst illegal taxes,
And by opposing end them.

The Massachusetts Spy, 1770

But as might have been observed, that it would require a great number of years, and many contingent events, to reconcile the inhabitants of the United States to the taxing of houses, lands, hearths, windowlights, and all the conveniences of life, as in England. Not the necessity of extracting themselves from old foreign debts, nor newly contracted expenses for exigencies or projects, which they had considered unnecessary in a republican government, could suddenly lead a people generally to acquiesce in measures, to which they had heretofore been strangers. The artificial creation of expenses by those who deem a public department a public blessing, will easily suggest plausible pretenses for taxation, until every class is burdened to the utmost stretch of forbearance, and the great body of the people reduced to penury and slavery.

Mercy Warren, 1805

They who feel the benefit ought to feel the burden.

John Dickinson, 1768

Taxes in every free state have been, and ought to be, as exactly proportioned as is possible to the abilities of those who are to pay them. They cannot other wise be just. Even a Hottentot would comprehend the unreasonableness of making a poor man pay as much for "defending" the property of a rich man, as the rich man pays himself.

John Dickinson, 1768

That the people should entertain the highest disgust of a board, instituted to superintend a revenue to be raised from them without their consent is natural.

James Otis, 1769

I was told that Friends in England frequently paid taxes when the money was applied to such purposes. I had conference with several noted Friends on the subject, who all favored the payment of such taxes . . . I all along believed that there were some upright-hearted men who paid such taxes, but could not see that their example was a sufficient reason for me to do so while I believed that the spirit of truth required of me, as an individual, to suffer patiently the distress of goods rather than pay actively. To refuse the active payment of a tax which our society generally paid was exceedingly disagreeable; but to do a thing contrary to my conscience appeared yet more dreadful . . . From the steady opposition which faithful Friends in early times made to wrong things then approved of, they were hated and persecuted by men living in the spirit of this world, and, suffering with firmness, they were made a blessing to the church, and the work prospered. It equally concerns men in every age to take heed to their own spirit.

John Woolman (on the war tax), 1750s

And we shall also free ourselves from those unmannerly pillagers who impudently tell us, that they are licensed by an act of Parliament to thrust their dirty hands into the pockets of every American.

John Hancock, 1774

THE LAND AND THE FARMER

For as long as the products of our labor, and the rewards of our care, can properly be called our own, so long it will be worth our while to be industrious and frugal. But if when we plow-sow-reap-gather-and thresh, and we find, that we plow-sow-reap-gather-and thresh for others, whose pleasure is to be the sole limitation how much they shall take, and how much they shall leave, why should we repeat the unprofitable toil? Horses and oxen are content with that portion of the fruits of their work which their owners assign them, in order to keep them strong enough to raise successive crops; but even these beasts will not submit to draw for their masters, until they are subdued by whips and goads.

John Dickinson, 1768

Those who labor in the earth are the chosen people of God, if ever he had a chosen people.

Thomas Jefferson, *Notes on Virginia*, 1782

The earth is given as a common stock to man to labor and live on. If, for the encouragement of industry we allow it to be appropriated, we must take care that other employment be permitted to those excluded from appropriation. If we do not, the fundamental right to labor the earth returns to the unemployed.

Thomas Jefferson, 1785

No man is entitled to a greater portion of the earth than another . . . (Land) was made for the use of all.

Pennsylvania Farmers, 1740s

The greatest service which can be rendered any country is to add an useful plant to its culture.

Thomas Jefferson

. . . the earth in its uncultivated state was, and ever would have continued to be, the common property of the human race.

Tom Paine, 1776

Farmers whose interests are entirely agricultural . . .
are the true representatives of the great American
interest, and are alone to be relied on for expressing
the proper American sentiments.

Thomas Jefferson, 1796

The idle, clerical, military, banking, loaning and
ennobled classes, as have been stated, have the
effect of raising prices very considerably; but the
agriculturists, who pay and maintain these classes,
still lose more than they gain.

John Taylor

Man did not make the earth, and though he had a
natural right to occupy it, he had no right to locate as
his property in perpetuity, any part of it.

Tom Paine, 1796

Corruption of morals in the mass of cultivators is a
phenomenon of which no age nor nation has furnished an example.

Thomas Jefferson

THE ISSUES
OF A DEMOCRACY

LAW AND ORDER

Where tyranny begins government ends.

Samuel West, 1776

Their wickedness breaks out, and one murder after another is committed under the connivance and encouragement even of that authority by which such crimes ought to be punished, that the purposes of oppression and despotism may be answered.

Samuel Langdon, 1775

Those who do not scruple to bring poverty, misery, slavery, and death upon thousands, will not hesitate at the most diabolical crimes.

Abigail Adams, 1774

That country is totally enslaved, where one single law can be made or repealed, without the consent of the people.

Benjamin Church, 1773

Law was the rule for courts and magistrates in the execution of their offices, but justice was our guide. It was a maxim that rigid law was rigid injustice.

William Maclay, 1790

Nothing but the infinite number of our laws and what is quoted as authority in our courts, together with the perplexity and confusion, gave these gentlemen their importance, or indeed any importance at all.

Christopher Gadsden, 1782

Nothing can be politically right, that is morally wrong; and no necessity can ever sanctify a law, that is contrary to equity.

Benjamin Rush, 1786

The law gives no indulgence to malice and rancour against any individual, much less against a community or the human species. He who threatens or thirsts for the blood of the community is an enemy to the public.

Sam Adams, 1770

And the laws already made, as they will be executed by officers altogether dependent on the Crown, will undoubtedly be perverted in the worst purposes. The governor of the province and the principal fortress in it are probably already thus supported. These are the first fruits of the system. If the rest should follow, it would be only in a greater degree, a violation of our essential, natural rights. For what purpose then will it be to preserve the old forms without the substance?

Massachusetts House of Representatives to Benjamin Franklin, 1771

Fidelity to the public requires that the laws be as plain and explicit as possible, that the less knowing may understand, and not be ensnarled by them, while the artful evade their force.

Samuel Cooke, 1770

Whatever the apparent cause of any riots may be, the real one is always want of happiness. It shows that something is wrong in the system of government that injures the felicity by which society is to be preserved.

Tom Paine, 1792

No usage, law, or authority whatever is so binding that it need or ought to be continued when it may be changed with advantage to the community. The prerogatives of the Crown . . . are only so many laws, mutable like other laws; whenever expediency requires, either by an ordinary act of the legislature, or if the situation deserved it, by the interposition of the people.

Tom Paine

If they become arbitrary and use their power against the people who give it, can they suppose that the people in their turn will not use their inherent power against their oppressors, and be as arbitrary as they? When such power is raised, as it is not under the restraint of any regular government or direction, terrible results may generally be expected from it. But those who are answerable for those results are those who raised the tempest. Let no man then suffer his rights to be torn from him for fear of the consequences of defending them—however dreadful they may be, the guilt of them does not lie at his door.

William Goddard,
The Constitutional Courant, 1765

When the people are oppressed, when their rights are infringed, when their property is invaded, when taskmasters are set over them, when unconstitutional acts are executed by a naval force before their eyes, and they are, daily threatened with military troops, when their legislature is dissolved—and what government is left is secret as a Divan—when placemen and their underlings swarm about them . . . in such circumstances the people will be discontented, and they are not to be blamed: their minds will be irritated as long as they have any sense of honor, liberty and virtue. In such circumstances, while they have the spirit of freedom, they will boldly assert their freedom; and they are to be justified in so doing. I know very well that to murmur, or even whisper a complaint, some people call it a riotous spirit. But they are in the right of it to complain, and complain ALOUD. And they will complain, till they are either redressed, or become poor, deluded, miserable, ductile dupes, fitted to be made the slaves of dirty tools of arbitrary power.

Sam Adams

A bill of rights is what the people are entitled to against every government on earth, general or particular, and what no just government should refuse, or rest on inference.

Thomas Jefferson, 1787

We, who are returned by the several towns in this county, to serve as grand jurors at the superior court for this present term, being actuated by a zealous regard for peace and good order, and a sincere desire to promote justice, righteousness and good government, as being essential to the happiness of the community, would now most gladly proceed to the discharge of the important duty required in that department, could we persuade ourselves that, by doing thus, it would add to our own reputation or promote the welfare of our country. But when we consider the dangerous inroads that have been made upon our civil constitution, the violent attempts now making to alter and annul the most essential parts of our charter, granted by the most solemn faith of kings, and repeatedly recognized by British kings and parliaments; while we see the open and avowed design of establishing the most complete system of despotism in this province and thereby reducing the free-born inhabitants thereof to the most abject state of slavery and bondage; we feel ourselves necessarily constrained to decline being impaneled, for reasons that we are ready to offer to the court. Three of the judges . . . are sworn to carry into execution all the late grievous acts of the British Parliament, among the last of which is one, made ostensibly for the impartial administration of justice in this province, but as we fear, really for the impunity of such persons as shall, under pretext of executing those acts, murder any of the inhabitants. These acts appear to us to be utterly repugnant to every idea of justice and common humanity, and are justly complained of, throughout America, as highly injurious and oppressive to the good people of this province and manifestly destructive of their natural as well as constitutional rights. Because we believe, in our consciences, that our acting in concert with a court so constituted, and under such circumstances, would be so far betraying the just and sacred rights of our native land, which were not the gifts of kings but were purchased solely with the toil, the blood, and treasure of our worthy and revered ancestors, and which we look upon ourselves under the most sacred obligations to maintain, and to transmit whole and entire to our posterity. Therefore, we unanimously decline serving as grand jurors at this court.

> Statement by twenty-two Bostonians
> including Paul Revere, 1774

The Revolutionary War

THE MILITARY

No man can pretend to say that the peace and good order of the community is so secure with soldiers quartered in the body of a city as without them. Besides, where military power is introduced, military maxims are propagated and adopted, which are inconsistent with and must soon eradicate every idea of civil government. Do we not already find some persons weak enough to believe, that an officer is obliged to obey the orders of his superiors, though it be even AGAINST the law?

Sam Adams, *Boston Gazette*, 1768

A standing army, in the time of profound peace is naturally productive of uneasiness and discontent among the people.

Letter to Dennis de Berdt, Esq., agent for the House of Representatives from the Province of Massachusetts Bay, 1768

An uncontrollable military power will never be established here. It never can, while the people entertain a just idea of the nature of civil government and are upon their guard against the daring encroachments of arbitrary, despotic power.

Sam Adams, 1771

Tyrants always support themselves with standing armies! And if possible the people are disarmed.

Samuel Webster, 1777

Even in the public military service, or warlike expeditions by national authority, the law manifestly requires the soldier to think for himself; to consider before he acts in any war, whether the same be just, for, if it be otherwise, the Common Law of the kingdom will impute to him guilty of murder.

Granville Sharp, 1773

It is the inherent right of every free man to vote and elect the officers who are to command them in a military character, and he who dares to attempt a contravention of the right forfeits all protection from this country, is a tyrant and a despot, and an enemy of the people.

Resolution of the Franklin Society of Pendleton, South Carolina

The spirit of this country is totally adverse to a large military force.

Thomas Jefferson, 1807

Soldiers are taught to consider arms as the only arbiters by which every dispute is to be decided . . . They are instructed implicitly to obey their commanders without enquiring into the justice of the cause they are engaged to support; hence it is, that they are ever to be dreaded as the ready engines of tyranny and oppression.

Joseph Warren, 1772

Among the officers of the British Army, the slavish maxim, "The will of the prince is law" too much prevails. They will suffer the arbitrary and cruel commands of their sovereign to supersede the dictates of honor, morality and conscience.

Sam Adams, 1775

He has affected to render the military independent of and superior to the civil power . . . He is, at this time, transporting large armies of foreign mercenaries to complete the works of death, desolation, and tyranny, already begun with circumstances of cruelty and perfidy, scarcely paralleled in the most barbarous ages, and totally unworthy of the head of a civilized nation.

> The Declaration of Independence, 1776

A standing army, however necessary it may be at some times, is always dangerous to the liberties of the people. Soldiers are apt to consider themselves as a body distinct from the rest of the citizens. They have their arms always in their hands. Their rules and their discipline is severe. They soon become attached to their officers and disposed to yield implicit obedience to their commands. Such a power should be watched with a jealous eye. I have a good opinion of the principal officers of our army; I esteem them as patriots as well as soldiers. But if this war continues, as it may, for years yet to come, we know not who may succeed them. Men who have been long governed by military laws and inured to military customs and habits may lose the spirit and feeling of citizens.

> Sam Adams, 1770

My God; What can this writer have in view by recommending such measures? Can he be a friend to the army? Can he be a friend to this country? Rather is he not an insidious foe?. . . Let me conjure you in the name of our common country, as you value your sacred honor, as you respect the rights of humanity, and as you regard the military and national character of America, to express your utmost horror and detestation of the man who wishes, under any specious pretences, to overturn the liberties of our country.

> George Washington (on reading of a proposal that he proclaim himself military dictator), 1782

The great oppressors of the earth were entrusted with power by the people to defend them from the little oppressors. The sword of justice was put into their hands, but behold they soon turned it into a sword of oppression . . . And so, in a multitude of instances, the remedy has proved unspeakably worse than the disease . . .

Samuel Webster, 1777

A writer of celebrity has observed, that "military commanders acquiring fame, and accustomed to receive the obedience of armies are in their hearts generally enemies to the popular equality of republics." Thus, the first step taken in the United States for the aggrandizement of particular families by distinguished orders, and assumed nobility, appeared to originate in the army; some of whom, as observed of the ancient barons of England, "soon forgot the cause and the patriotism of their ancestors, and insensibly became the servants of luxury and government."

Mercy Warren, 1805

The greatest happiness of the greatest number being the object and bond of society, the establishment of truth and justice ought to be the basis of civil policy and jurisprudence. But this capital establishment can never be attained in a state where there exists a power superior to the civil magistrate and sufficient to control the authority of the laws.

Josiah Quincy, 1774

Though it has been said that a standing army is necessary for the dignity and safety of America, freedom revolts at the idea. Standing armies have been the nursery of vice and the bane of liberty from the Roman legions to the planting of British cohorts in the capitals of America.

Mercy Warren, 1788

FOREIGN AFFAIRS

See the bright flame arise
In yonder eastern skies,
Spreading in veins.
Tis pure Democracy
Setting all nations free
Melting our chains.

Joseph Coswell, *Ode to Liberty*, 1793

Justice is as strictly due between neighbor nations
as between neighbor citizens. A highwayman is as
much a robber when he plunders in a gang as when
single; and a nation that makes an unjust war is only
a *great gang*.

Benjamin Franklin, 1785

A just and solid republican government maintained
here will be a standing monument and example for
the aim and imitation of the people of other countries; and I join with you in the hope and belief that
they will see from our example that a free government is of all others the most energetic; that the
enquiry which has been excited among the mass of
mankind by our revolution and its consequences,
will ameliorate the condition of man over a great
portion of the globe . . . What a satisfaction have we
in the contemplation of the benevolent effects of our
efforts compared with those of the leaders of the
other side, who have discountenanced all advances
in science as dangerous innovations, have endeavored

to render philosophy and republicanism terms of reproach, to persuade us that man cannot be governed but by the rod, etc. I shall have the happiness of dying in the contrary hope.

Thomas Jefferson, 1801

I beg leave to recommend to you in general as the best method of attaining this wisdom—diligently to study the histories of other countries. You will there find all the arts that can possibly be practiced by cunning rulers, or false patriots among yourselves, so fully delineated, that, changing names, the account would serve for your own times.

John Dickinson, 1768

The first great object is to convince the people of the importance of their present situation: for the majority of a great people, on a subject which they understand will never act wrong. Every citizen of the American empire ought now to consider himself as the legislator of half mankind. He will see that the system to be established by his suffrage, is calculated for the great benevolent purposes of extending peace, happiness, and progressive improvement to a large proportion of his fellow creatures.

Joel Barlow, 1787

When we take a survey of mankind, we cannot help cursing the wretch who, to the unavoidable misfortunes of nature, shall willfully add the calamities of war. One would think there were evils enough in the world without studying to increase them, and that life is sufficiently short without shaking the sand that measures it.

Tom Paine, *The Crisis*, No. 5, 1778

I join with you most cordially in rejoicing at the return of peace. I hope it will be lasting, and that mankind will at length, as they call themselves reasonable creatures, have reason to settle their differences without cutting throats; for, in my opinion, there never was a good war, or a bad peace.

Benjamin Franklin, 1783

A pretty pass of society we have already arrived at! It would be much more consonant to the dignity of Congress to establish a spirited inquiry how we came to be involved in a war without the authority of Congress than to be begging our own servants to spare the effusion of human blood!

William Maclay, 1791

Our enemies give us opprobrious names; they call us insurgents and rebels . . . We conjure you by that friendship which has so long subsisted between us, by the blood and sufferings we have exhibited in your cause, by your own honor and liberties, which are at stake, to rise and crush that spirit of oppression now exercised in seeking our destruction. Be assured that if you suffer us tamely to be devoured by those greedy powers who have laid plans for our ruin, that spirit will not sleep long before you fare the same fate; for we conceive the liberties of the whole to be absolutely connected with every part of an empire founded on the common rights of mankind.

Vermont's *Appeal to the World*, 1779

God grant, that not only the love of liberty, but a thorough knowledge of the rights of man may pervade all the nations of the earth, so that a philosopher may set his foot anywhere on its surface and say, 'This is my country . . .'

Benjamin Franklin, 1790

It would be unfortunate were it in the power of any one man to defeat the issue of so beautiful a revolution. I hope and trust it is not, and that for the good of suffering humanity all over the earth, that revolution will be established and spread through the whole world.

Thomas Jefferson (on the French Revolution), 1791

Over the foreign powers I am convinced they will triumph completely, and I cannot but hope that that triumph, and the consequent disgrace of the invading tyrants, is destined, in order of events, to kindle the wrath of the people of Europe against those who have dared to embroil them in such wickedness, and to bring at length kings, nobles and priests to the scaffolds they have been so long deluging with human blood.

Thomas Jefferson (on the French Revolution)

To the lovers of freedom throughout the world.
To the unfortunate but gallant people of Ireland—May their ardour for liberty never subside until they have thrown off the chains of oppression with which they have been bound nearly six hundred years.
To the persecuted of all nations.
To persecuted patriots throughout the world—Fall, tyrants . . . Fall!
To liberty and equality—the universal law of nations.
To the republicans of the old world—As long as kings shall be the mark, may they never miss their aim.
May the tyrants of the earth soon cease to tyrannize over their fellow creatures, and learn to know all men are born equal.

July 4th Toast of the 1790 s

The means and the measures (of the Revolution) are the proper objects of investigation. These may be of use to posterity, not only in this nation, but in South America and all other countries.

John Adams, 1818

In the name and behalf of all the true Sons of Liberty in America, Great Britain, Ireland, Corsica, or wheresoever they may be dispersed throughout the world.

Dedication of the Providence, Rhode Island, Liberty Tree, 1768

EDUCATION

Where learning is confined to a few people, we always find monarchy, aristocracy and slavery.

Benjamin Rush, 1786

A nation under a well-regulated government should permit none to remain uninstructed. It is monarchial and aristocratic governments, only, that require ignorance for their support.

Tom Paine, *Rights of Man,* 1792

It is a well-known fact, that persons unfriendly to the Revolution, were always most numerous in those parts of the United States which had either never been illuminated, or but faintly warmed by the rays of science. The uninformed and the misinformed, constituted a great proportion of those Americans who preferred the leading strings of the parent state, though encroaching on their liberties, to a government of their own countrymen and fellow citizens.

David Ramsay, 1789

. . . there are two ways of governing mankind; by keeping them ignorant, (or) by making them wise. The former was and is the custom of the old world. The latter of the new.

Tom Paine, 1778

If science produces no better fruits than tyranny, murder, rapine and destitution of national morality, I would rather wish our country to remain ignorant.

Thomas Jefferson

Liberty cannot be preserved without a general knowledge among the people.

John Adams, 1767

Knowledge and learning may well be considered as most essentially requisite to a free righteous government. A republican government and science mutually promote and support each other.

Phillips Payson, 1778

. . . it is the practice of the new world, America, to make men as wise as possible, so that their knowledge being complete, they may be rationally governed.

Tom Paine, 1778

Enlighten the people generally, and tyranny and oppressions of body and mind will vanish like evil spirits at the dawn of day.

Thomas Jefferson, 1816

Imagination can scarce paint the superior condition of that state where learning, science, and the liberal arts flourish, to that of a rude and unpolished people.

Noah Webster, 1763

Upon the whole, it appears that whether the design be to preserve a good constitution, civil and religious, and transmit its spirit uncorrupted down through the ages, or whether the design be to mend a bad one and secure it against all dangers from without, it is only to be done effectually by the slow but sure means of a proper education of youth.

Francis Hopkinson (at age 16), 1754

When sobered by experience, I hope our successors will turn their attention to the advantages of education. I mean of education on the broad scale, and not that of the petty academies.

Thomas Jefferson, 1814

The general spread of the light of science has already laid open to every view the palpable truth that the mass of mankind has not been born with saddles on their backs nor a favored few booted and spurred, ready to ride them legitimately, by the grace of God. These are grounds of hope for others.

Thomas Jefferson

Neither piety, virtue, or liberty can long flourish in a community where the education of youth is neglected.

Samuel Cooper, 1780

Learning is both nurse and offspring of public-spirit.

Noah Webster, 1763

There is but one method of preventing crimes, and of rendering a republican form of government durable, and that is by disseminating the seeds of virtue and knowledge through every part of the state, by means of proper modes and places of education, and this can be done effectually only, by the interference and aid of the legislature.

Benjamin Rush, 1786

It is a shame, a scandal to civilized society, that part only of the citizens should be sent to colleges and universities, to learn to cheat the rest of their liberties.

Robert Coram, 1791

Let the people by all means encourage schools and colleges, and all the means of learning knowledge.

Samuel Webster, 1777

The preservation of the means of knowledge among the lowest ranks is of more importance to the public than all the property of all the rich men in the country.

John Adams, 1765

FREE PRESS AND FREE SPEECH

. . . no government ought to be without critics and where the press is free no one ever will. If (the government) is virtuous, it need not fear the free operation of attack and defense. Nature has given man no other means of sifting out the truth, either in religion, law or politics . . .

Thomas Jefferson, 1791

The liberty of the press is essential to the security of freedom in a state. It ought not, therefore, be restrained in this Commonwealth.

Massachusetts Bill of Rights, 1780

I entirely agree with you that an interest in the public prints is of great importance. The spirit of liberty would soon be lost and the people would grow quite lethargic, if there was not some one on watch, to waken and rouse them.

Andrew Eliot, 1776

The only security of all is a free press. The force of public opinion cannot be resisted, when permitted freely to be expressed. The agitation it produces must be submitted to. It is necessary to keep the waters pure.

Thomas Jefferson, 1823

The liberty of the press is a great bulwark of the
liberty of the people: It is therefore the incumbent
duty of those who are constituted the guardians of
the people's right, to defend and maintain it.

> Massachusetts House of
> Representatives, 1768

To the press alone, checkered as it is with abuses,
the world is indebted for all the triumphs which have
been obtained by reason and humanity over error
and oppression.

> James Madison, 1799

It is a principle among printers, that when truth has
fair play, it will always prevail over falsehood; therefore, though they have an undoubted property in
their own press, yet they willingly allow that anyone
is entitled to the use of it, who thinks it necessary
to offer his sentiments on disputable points to the
public, and will be at the expense of it. If what is
published be good, mankind has the benefit of it: If
it be bad the more tis made public the more its
weakness be exposed, and the greater disgrace falls
on the author, whoever he be; who is at the same
time deprived of an advantage he would otherwise
without fail make use of, viz. of complaining, *that
the truth is suppressed, and that he could say
MIGHTY MATTERS had he but the opportunity of
being heard.*

> Benjamin Franklin, 1740

In establishing American independence, the pen and
the press had merit equal to that of the sword.

> David Ramsay, 1783

Care has been taken that the art of printing should
be encouraged, and that it should be easy and cheap
and safe for any person to communicate his thoughts
to the public.

> Jeremy Gridley, 1767

Were it left for me to decide whether we should have a government without newspapers, or newspapers without a government, I should not hesitate a moment to prefer the latter.

Thomas Jefferson, 1787

I have lent myself willingly as the subject of a great experiment . . . to demonstrate the falsehood of the pretext that freedom of the press is incompatible with orderly government.

Thomas Jefferson, 1807

Should the liberty of the press be once destroyed, farewell the remainder of our invaluable rights and privileges! We may next expect padlocks on our lips, fetters on our legs, and only our hands at liberty to slave for our worse than Egyptian taskmasters, or fight our way to constitutional freedom.

Isaiah Thomas

. . . a citizen of the United States comes forward, with his name, and produces charges against a *public character*—surely in such a case, with the smallest pretensions to a free and impartial and a patriotic press, surely such publication ought not to be rejected.

The Federal Gazette, 1792

I am really mortified to be told that, in the United States of America, a fact like this can become a subject of inquiry, and of criminal inquiry too . . . that a question about the sale of a book can be carried before the civil magistrates . . . Are we to have a censor whose imprimatur shall say what books may be sold, and what we may buy? . . . It is an insult to our citizens to question whether they are rational beings or not.

Thomas Jefferson, 1814

An evil magistrate, entrusted with a power to punish words, is armed with a weapon the most destructive and terrible. Under the pretense of pruning off the exuberant branches, he frequently destroys the tree.

James Alexander, 1735

WOMEN

I know this, that as free I can die but once, but as a slave I shall not be worthy of life. I have the pleasure to assure you that these are the sentiments of all my sister Americans. They have sacrificed both assemblies, parties of pleasure, tea drinking and finery to that great spirit of patriotism, that actuates all ranks and degrees of people throughout this extensive continent. They are as with one heart determined to die or be free.

Letter from a woman to
a British officer, 1775

I cannot say, that I think you are very generous to the ladies; for, whilst you are proclaiming peace and goodwill to men, emancipating all nations, you insist upon retaining an absolute power over wives. But you must remember, that arbitrary power is like most other things which are very hard, very liable to be broken; and, notwithstanding all your wise laws and maxims, we have it in our power, not only to free ourselves, but to subdue our masters, and, without violence, throw both your natural and legal authority at our feet.

Abigail Adams, 1776

He is very saucy to me in return for a list of female grievances which I transmitted to him. I think I will get you to join me in a petition to Congress. I thought it was very probable our wise statesmen would erect a new government and form a new code of laws. I ventured to speak a word in behalf of our sex, who are rather hardly dealt with by the laws of England, which gives such unlimited power to the husband to use his wife ill. I requested that our legislators would consider our case. And as all men of delicacy and sentiment are averse to exercising the power they possess, yet—as there is a natural propensity in human nature to domination, I thought the most generous plan was to put it out of the power of the arbitrary and tyrannic to injure us with impunity, by establishing some laws in our favor upon just and liberal principles.

> Abigail Adams (to Mercy Warren), 1776

When and where was the original compact for introducing government into any society made? Who were present and parties to such compacts? Who acted for infants and women? . . . Are not women as free as men? Would it not be infamous to assert that the ladies are all slaves by nature?

> James Otis, 1764

Nothing has been more injurious than the separation of the sexes. They associate in childhood without restraint; but the period quickly arrives when they are obliged to take different paths. She will be most applauded when she smiles with most perseverance on her oppressor, and when, with the undistinguishing attachment of a dog, no caprice or cruelty shall be able to estrange her affection.

> The male character of Charles Brown's *Alcuin*, 1798

I can hear of the brilliant accomplishments of any of my sex with pleasure, and rejoice in that liberality of sentiment which acknowledges them. . . . But, in this country, you need not be told how much female education is neglected, nor how fashionable it has been to ridicule female learning. If women are to be esteemed our enemies, methinks it is an ignoble cowardice, thus to disarm them, and not allow them the same weapons we use ourselves; but, if they deserve the title of our friends, 'tis an inhuman tyranny to debar them of the privileges of ingenuous education, which would tender their friendship so much more delightful to themselves and us.

Abigail Adams, 1778

If particular care and attention are not paid to the ladies we are determined to foment a rebellion and will not hold ourselves bound to obey any laws in which we have no voice or representation.

Abigail Adams, 1776

The influence of female education upon morals, taste and patriotism should not be passed over in silence.

Benjamin Rush, 1811

The women, both old and young, being greatly irritated at the inflexibility of administration, are not only willing their sons and brothers should turn out in the field, but also declare that they will give them up and themselves likewise as a sacrifice before they will bow to Pharaoh's task-masters; this makes the raising of troops on the continent very easy. Let a person go into any province, city, or county, and ask the females, "Are you willing your sons or brothers should go for soldiers and defend their liberties?" they would severally answer, "Yes, with all my soul, and if they won't go I won't own them as my sons, or brothers; for I'll help myself if there should be any need of mine. If I can't stand in the ranks, I can help forward with powder, balls and provisions." This, my lord, is the language of the American women.

Maryland minister writing to
Lord Dartmouth

The women amuse themselves by teaching their children the principles of rebellion, and seem to take care that the rising generation should be as troublesome as themselves.

> British officer writing about women prisoners in Charleston, 1780

While I am conscious of being an intelligent and moral being; while I see myself denied, in so many cases, the exercise of my own discretion; incapable of separate property; subject in all periods of my life, to the will of another, on whose bounty I am made to depend for food, raiment, and shelter; when I see myself in my relation to society, regulated merely as a beast, or an insect; passed over, in the distribution of public duties, as absolutely nothing, by those who disdain to assign the least apology for their injustice—what though politicians say I am nothing, it is impossible I should assent to their opinion, as long as I am conscious of willing and moving. If they generously admit me into the class of existence, but affirm that I exist for no more purpose than the convenience of the more dignified sex; that I am not to be entrusted with the government of myself; that to foresee, to deliberate and decide, belongs to others while all my duties resolve themselves into this precept, "listen and obey", it is not for me to smile at their tyranny, or receive, as my gospel, a code built upon such atrocious maxims.

> The female character of Charles Brown's *Alcuin*, 1798

THE RIGHTS OF MINORITIES

It always appeared a most iniquitous scheme to me to fight ourselves for what we are daily robbing and plundering from those who have as good a right to freedom as we have.

> Abigail Adams, 1774

Is it not amazing that at a time when the rights of humanity are defined and understood with precision, in a country above all others fond of liberty, that in such an age and in such a country, we find men—professing a religion the most humane, mild, gentle and generous—adopting a principle as repugnant to humanity as it is inconsistent with the Bible and destructive of liberty? . . . I will not, I cannot justify it.

> Patrick Henry, 1773

Slavery is such an atrocious debasement of human nature that its very extirpation if not performed with solicitous care, may sometimes open a source of serious evils.

> Pennsylvania Society promoting "the Abolition of Slavery, and the Relief of Free Negroes," 1789

(The Massachusetts State Constitution of 1789) sees fit with declaring that all men are born free and equal—and that every subject is entitled to liberty . . . and in short is totally repugnant to the idea of being

born slaves. This being the case, I think the idea of
slavery is inconsistent with our own conduct and
Constitution.

William Cushing, 1781

A spirit of humanity and religion begins to awaken,
in several of the colonies in favour of the poor
Negroes.

Benjamin Rush, 1773

Does it follow that it is right to enslave a man because he is black? Will short curled hair, like wool
. . . help the argument? Can any logical inference in
favour of slavery be drawn from a flat nose, a long
or short face?

James Otis

We attempted indeed to form treaties with the
Indians, and to make (land) purchases. But in doing
this, we conducted ourselves rather as proprietors of
the soil than as purchasers, and prescribed certain
bounds beyond which we would suffer them to live.
These bounds were extended much further westward
than was yet necessary for our settlements, and was
therefore an unnecessary intrusion upon their room
for hunting, which is their means of subsistence.

George Mason, 1792

A perpetual alliance, offensive and defensive, is to
be entered into as soon as may be with the Six
(Indian) Nations; their limits to be ascertained and
secured to them; their land not to be encroached
on, nor any private or colony purchases made of
them hereafter to be held good, nor any contract
for lands to be made but between the Great Council
(of the Indians) at Onondaga and the General Congress . . .

Article X of the Articles
of Confederation, 1775

A Whig abhors the very idea of slavery, let the colour
or complexion of a slave be what it may. He is a

friend of liberty, and a supporter of the rights of mankind universally, without any regard to partial interests or selfish views.

New Jersey Gazette, 1780

We acknowledge our obligation to you for what you have already done, but as the people of this province seem to be actuated by the principles of equity and justice, we cannot but expect your house will again take our deplorable case into serious consideration, and give us that ample relief which, as men, we have a natural right to.

Circular Committee of
Slaves, 1773

REVOLUTIONARY TIMES

DAY-TO-DAY LIFE IN A REVOLUTION

You will find that the proceedings of our citizens have been united, spirited and firm. The flame is kindled and like lightning it catches from soul to soul.

Abigail Adams, 1773

The state of this province is a great curiosity. Four hundred thousand people are in a state of nature, and yet as still and peaceable at present as ever they were when government was in full vigor. We have neither legislators, nor magistrates, nor executive officers . . . The town of Boston is a spectacle worthy of the attention of a deity, suffering amazing distress yet determined to endure as much as human nature can, rather than betray America and posterity.

A letter from Boston, 1775

It is a great consolation to find that our friends in the country approve of the conduct of this and the neighboring towns at the late meetings. We are assured of this by the letters we almost daily receive. I think we have put our enemies in the wrong, and they must, in the judgement of rational men, be answerable for the destruction of the tea, which their own obstinacy had rendered necessary. Notwithstanding what your Tories have given out, the people here are universally pleased.

Sam Adams, 1773

You have doubtless observed in the newspapers the account they first received of our opposition to the 'East India Act,' as it is called, particularly the transactions at Liberty Tree, which they treated with sneer and ridicule. But when they heard of the resolves of the body of the people at the Old South meetinghouse . . . they put on grave countenances.

Sam Adams, 1774

Our enemies would intimidate us by saying our brethren in the other towns are indifferent about this matter.

Sam Adams, 1772

I must now give you joy on the diffusion of that noble spirit of liberty we have lately seen exhibited . . . I heartily wish a perseverance in the blissful path, and may every avaricious despot who aims at grasping all the good things with which heaven meant to bless mankind, be made sensible he is not the only figure of importance in the Creation.

Hannah Winthrop, 1773

Oh England, England, miserable grown,
Since he who has no brains enjoys thy throne.

Graffiti on inn wall, Coventry, England, 1760s

Glorious are the complaints of provisions of all sorts. Every post brings fresh accounts of tumults, occasioned principally by the high price of bread.

Pennsylvania Gazette, 1766

There are nothing but riots and insurrections over the whole country, on account of the high price of provisions, in particular, corn.

Pennsylvania Gazette, 1766

When the clergy engage in political warfare, religion becomes a most powerful engine, either to support or overthrow the state. What effect it must have had upon the audience, to hear the same sentiments and principles, which they had before read in a newspaper, delivered on Sundays from the sacred desk, with a religious awe and the most solemn appeals to Heaven, from lips which they had been taught from their cradles to believe could utter nothing but eternal truths!

David Leonard, *Massachusettensis*, 1774

I congratulate you on the union of sentiment and spirit prevailing through the continent, which makes even our Tory protestors hang their ears.

James Warren, 1774

We heartily join with you in wishing the glorious spirit of liberty which now animates the inhabitants of this province shall be diffused through the colonies and happily effect the restoration of their rights, which are cruelly ravished from them.

Boston Committee of Correspondence (to Lynn Committee of Correspondence), 1773

They are haughty and jealous of their liberties and can scarcely bear the thought of being controlled by any superior power.

A Frenchman visiting Virginia

A British soldier deserted to the rebels and helped them form a militia company of fifty men. One day, a sergeant and eight Redcoats came to apprehend him. He said, "You must know that we determine everything here by a vote," and turning to the rebels, asked if he should be arrested. The vote being fifty in the negative, the Redcoats outnumbered, decided to retreat to Boston. But two of the eight British privates, themselves, asked for a vote on whether they should desert, and received unanimous approval from the rebels. The sergeant and his remaining six men hastily departed.

John Trumbull, 1774

Undaunted by TYRANTS—we'll DIE or be FREE
Motto of *The Newport Mercury*, 1769

The ancients considered the snake or serpent as an emblem of wisdom, and of endless duration. The rattlesnake is properly a representative of America, as this animal is found in no other part of the world. The eye of the creature excels in brightness that of any other animal; she has no eyelids, and is therefore an emblem of vigilance. She never begins an attack, nor ever surrenders; she is therefore an emblem of magnanimity and courage.
When injured or in danger, she never wounds until she has given notice to the enemies of their danger; no other of her kind shows such generosity. When she is undisturbed, and in peace, she does not appear to be furnished with weapons of any kind; they are latent in the roof of her mouth, and even when extended for her defense, appear to those who are unacquainted with them to be weak and contemptible; yet their wounds, however small, are decisive and fatal.

A Virginian explaining why the rattlesnake of the "Don't Tread on Me" flag is the proper revolutionary symbol for America, 1776

The manner in which the war has been prosecuted has confirmed us in these sentiments; piracy and murder, robbery and breach of faith, have been conspicuous in the conduct of the King's troops: defenseless towns have been attacked and destroyed: the cries of the widow and the orphan demand our attention; they demand that the hand of pity should wipe the tear from their eye, and that the sword of their country should avenge their wrongs.

> Instructions of the Town of Malden, Massachusetts, to their representatives in Congress, 1776

PATRIOTS AND TORIES VIEW OUR FIRST
4TH OF JULY

Three cheers rended the welkin. The batallions paraded on the Common and gave us a *feu de joie*, notwithstanding the scarcity of powder. The bells rang all day and almost all night.

> John Adams (of the Philadelphia Celebration), 1776

The Declaration of Independence was the crown with which the people of United America, rising in gigantic stature as one man, encircled their brows, and there it remains; so long as this globe shall be inhabited by human beings, may it remain, a crown of imperishable glory!

> John Quincy Adams (4th of July oration), 1831

As we passed through the town, we found it
thronged; all were in their holiday suits; every eye
beamed with delight, and every tongue was in rapid
motion. The town clerk read from a balcony the
Declaration to the crowd, at the close of which a
shout began in the hall, passed to the streets, which
rang with loud huzzas, the slow and measured boom
of cannon, and the rattle of musketry.

> An imprisoned British officer
> (writing of the news of the
> Declaration in Boston), 1776

This afternoon the Declaration of Independence was
read at the head of each brigade of the Continental
Army . . . It was received everywhere with loud
huzzas and the utmost demonstrations of joy. And
tonight the equestrian statue of George III has, by
the Sons of Freedom, been laid prostrate in the dirt
—the just desert of our infatuated adversaries.

> New York newspaper account of the
> first reading of the Declaration of
> Independence, 1776

The general hopes that this important event will serve
as a fresh incentive to every officer and soldier to
act with fidelity and courage, as knowing that now
the peace and safety of his country depend solely
on the success of our arms.

> George Washington, 1776

I am well aware of the toil, and blood, and treasure
that it will cost to maintain this Declaration, and
support and defend these States. Yet, through all
this gloom, I can see the rays of ravishing light and
glory. I can see that the end is more than worth all
the means; and that our posterity will triumph in that
day's transaction.

> John Adams, 1776

The bells rang, the privateers fired the forts and batteries, the cannon were discharged . . . and every face appeared joyful . . . After dinner the King's arms were taken down from the State House and every vestige of him from every place . . . and burnt . . . Thus ends royal authority in this State, and all the people shall say Amen.

> Abigail Adams (of Boston Declaration reading), 1776

We commit his political existence to the ground—corruption to corruption—tyranny to the grave—and oppression to eternal infamy, in sure and certain hope that he will never obtain a resurrection, to rule again over the United States of America.

> Mock funeral oration for George III read upon the news of the Declaration, 1776

We dined under the cedar trees, and cheerfully drank to the United Free and Independent States of America. In the evening the town was illuminated, and there was exhibited a very solemn funeral procession, attended by the Grenadier and Light Infantry Companies, and other militia, with their drums muffled and fifes, and a greater number of people than ever appeared on any occasion before in this Province, when George III was interred before the court house.

> A newspaper account from Savannah, Georgia, 1776

The Declaration has had a glorious effect—it has made these colonies all alive.

> William Whipple, 1776

With the independence of these American states, a new era in politics has commenced. Our future happiness or misery, therefore, as a people, depend entirely on ourselves.

> Jonathan Elmer, 1776

Our Declaration of Independence has given wings to the spirits of the people.

Sam Adams, 1776

The spirit of liberty reigns triumphant in Pennsylvania.

Benjamin Rush, 1776

We have put on the harness, and I trust it will not be put off until we see our land a land of security and freedom—the wonder of the other hemisphere— the asylum of all who pant for deliverance from bondage.

Tristam Dalton, 1776

So daring and desperate is the spirit of those leaders, whose object has always been dominion and power . . If these treasons be suffered to take root, much mischief must grow from it . . .

George III, 1776

We cannot forbear to express our detestation and abhorance of the audacious and desperate spirit of ambition, which has at least carried those leaders, so far, as to make them openly renounce their allegiance. . .

House of Commons, 1776

We have lost America forever!

Whig Gazette, 1776

The Declaration of Independence was the first act that put an end to the administration of justice under the British Crown within the thirteen colonies. The revolt was now complete. Upon this event the law, the courts, and justice itself ceased; all was anarchy, all was confusion. A usurped kind of government took place, a medley of military law, convention ordinances, Congress recommendations and committee resolutions.

Thomas Jones

A new era in politics has commenced . . . No people under heaven were ever favored with a fairer opportunity of laying a sure foundation for future grandeur and happiness than we.

A New Jersey orator, 1776

May the Declaration of Independence be to the world what I believe it will be (to some parts sooner, to others later, but finally to all) the signal of arousing men to burst the chains under which monkish ignorance and superstition have persuaded them to bind themselves and assume the blessings and security of self-government.

Thomas Jefferson, 1826

TORIES LOOK AT OUR FOUNDERS

A most daring spirit of resistance and disobedience to the laws unhappily prevails in the province of Massachusetts, and has broken forth with fresh violence of a very criminal nature.

George III, 1774

I am, however, clearly of opinion that all power will quickly be transferred into the hands of the multitude, who, once taking the lead, will not easily be reduced again to proper submission.

William Eddis, 1775

The troubles began and put an end to everything that was pleasant and proper.

John Boucher, 1786

I think we should (whenever we get further into the country), give free liberty to the soldiers to ravage it at will, that these infatuated wretches may feel what a calamity war is.

British Army officer, 1776

And to the end that no person within the limits of this proffered mercy may plead ignorance of the consequences of refusing it, I by these presents proclaim, not only the persons above-named and excepted, but also all their adherents, associates and abettors, meaning to comprehend in those terms all and every person, and persons of what class, denomination or description soever, who have appeared in arms against the King's government, and shall not lay down the same as afore-mentioned; and likewise all such as shall so take arms after the date hereof, or who shall in anywise protect and conceal such offenders or assist them with money, provision, cattle, arms, ammunition, carriages, or any other necessary for subsistence or offense; or shall hold secret correspondence with them by letter, message, signal or otherwise, to be rebels and traitors, and as such to be treated.

Thomas Gage, 1775

The dirty mob was all about me as I drove into town.

Peggy Hutchinson

Whereas the infatuated multitudes, who have long suffered themselves to be conducted by certain well-known incendiaries and traitors, in a fatal progression of crimes, against the constitutional authority of that state, have at length proceeded to avowed rebellion; and the good effects which were expected to arise from the patience and lenience of the King's government, have been often frustrated, and are now rendered hopeless, by the influence of the same evil councils; it only remains for those who are entrusted with supreme rule, as well for the punishment of the guilty, as the protection of the well affected, to prove they do not bear the sword in vain.

Thomas Gage, Proclamation, 1775

The die is now cast, the colonies must either submit or triumph. I do not wish to come to severer measures, but we must not retreat; by coolness and unremitted pursuit of the measures that have been adopted I trust they will come to submit.

George III, 1774

The rebels (in Boston) have lately amused themselves with burning the houses on an island just under the admiral's nose; and a schooner with four carriage-guns and some swivels, which he sent to drive them off, unfortunately got ashore, and the rebels burned her.

Hugh Percy, 1775

In this province we are more unhappily circumstanced than in any other, for there are very few men of real abilities, gentlemen, or men of property, in their Whig tribunals. The parochial Committee are a parcel of the lowest people, chiefly carpenters, shoemakers, blacksmiths, etc., with a Jew at their head (Mordecai Sheftall, a merchant); in the General Committee, and Council of Safety, there are some better sort of men, and some merchants and planters—but many of the inferior class, and it is really terrible, my Lord, that such people should be suffered to overturn civil government.

William Wright, 1775

Many thought they could not be friends to their country, unless they trod in the same steps and imitated the example of the Bostonians.

A Tory, 1774

The press, that distinguished appendage of public liberty, and when fairly and impartially employed, its best support, has been invariably prostituted to the most contrary purposes: the animated language of ancient and virtuous times, calculated to vindicate and promote the just rights and interests of mankind, have been applied to countenance the most abandoned violation of those sacred blessings; and not only from the flagitious prints, but from the popular harangues of the times, men have been taught to depend upon activity in treason for the security of their persons and properties; till, to complete the horrible profanation of terms and of ideas, the name of God has been introduced in the pulpits to excite and justify devastation and massacre.

Thomas Gage, 1775

The offense of the Americans is flagitious. The town of Boston ought to be knocked about its ears and destroyed. You will never meet with proper obedience to the laws of this country until you have destroyed that nest of locusts.

Speech by a member of
Parliament, 1774

OUR FOUNDERS LOOK AT TORIES

I am pleased with the measures you are taking with the Tories. Don't let the execution of the good law be abated an iota in a single instance. If they take the oath, you must nevertheless keep a watchful eye over them. They are a cursed generation. We are plagued with them here beyond bearing.

Sam Adams, 1777

We, therefore, declare that whatever punishment shall be inflicted upon any persons in the power of our enemies for favoring, aiding or abetting the cause of American liberty, shall be retaliated in the same kind, and in the same degree upon those in power, who have favoured, aided or abetted, or shall favour, aid or abet the system of ministerial oppression.

> Declaration of the Thirteen
> United Colonies, in Congress,
> 1775

I heartily wish every Tory were extirpated from America; they are continually, by secret means, undermining and injuring our cause.

> Abigail Adams, 1776

Whereas Israel Rogers, one of the disarmed (Tories) in this district, being since charged with counteracting the measures carrying on for the preservation of American liberty; we do hereby strictly enjoin all manner of persons in this District, immediately to break off every kind of civil, mechanical, and commercial intercourse with this deluded and obstinate person, as they will answer the contrary at their peril.

> Committee of Safety of
> Great Neck, New York,
> 1776

... the 217 that have fallen to our (Virginia) share are distributed through this Colony, a few in each county, and permitted to hire themselves out to labour, thus to become citizens of America instead of its enemies.

> Richard Henry Lee (of
> captured Royal sailors),
> 1776

Resolved that James Christie has manifested a spirit and principle altogether inimical to the rights and liberties of America; that the said James Christie, by insinuating the necessity of introducing a military force into this province, has manifested an inveterate enmity to the liberty of this province in particular, and of British America in general. Therefore, resolved, that the said James Christie is and ought to be considered as an enemy to America, and that no person trade, deal, or barter with him hereafter, unless for necessaries and provisions, or for the sale or purchase of any part of his real or personal estate, of which he may be at this time seized or possessed. Resolved, that the said James Christie be expelled and banished from this province forever, and that he depart the province before the first day of September next.

> Maryland Committee of Safety, 1775

May the tories enjoy,
Without any alloy,
The slavery on us they would bring.
In sorrow and care
Till death let them wear
The chains of that tyrant, their king.

> A ballad, 1778

What a spirit of contradiction and toryism do we see prevailing! How often do we see people blind to their own interests, precipitately madding on to their own destruction.

> Hannah Winthrop, 1773

Pro Patria. The first Man that either distributes or makes use of stamped paper let him take care of his house, person, and effects. *Vox Populi.* We Dare!

> Anti-Stamp Act broadside, 1765

It having been thought highly expedient, at this exigency of our public affairs, that every person among us who is known to be an enemy to the rights and privileges of this country, and has been aiding and abetting the cursed plans of a tyrannical ruler, and an abandoned ministry, should be disarmed and rendered as incapable as possible of doing further material mischief, the Tories in Worcester, Massachusetts, were notified to appear with their arms and ammunitions on Monday last. They accordingly appeared, and after surrendering their arms to the Committee of Correspondence, and being strictly ordered not to leave town, or to meet together without a permit, were dismissed.

Newspaper account, 1775

A Tory here is the most despicable animal in the creation: Spiders, toads, snakes are their only proper emblem.

John Adams, 1774

We had some grand Tory rides in this city this week and in particular yesterday. Several of them were handled very roughly being carried through the streets on rails, their clothes torn from their backs and their bodies pretty well mingled with the dust. There is hardly a Tory face to be seen this morning.

Peter Elting, 1776

One or two have done what a great number ought to have done long ago—committed suicide. By all accounts there never existed a more miserable set of beings than these wretched creatures now are.

George Washington, 1776

MAKING HISTORY

Our affairs are hastening fast to a crisis, and the approaching campaign will, in all probability, determine forever the fate of America.

John Hancock, 1774

We live in a most important age, which demands that every moment should be improved to some serious purpose. And to do justice to our most gracious King, I will affirm it as my opinion that his councils and administration will necessarily produce the grandest revolutions the world has ever seen. Events succeed each other so rapidly that the most industrious and able politicians can scarcely improve them to the full purposes for which they seem to be designed.

Sam Adams, 1775

The question is not "whether some branches shall be lopped off." The axe is laid to the root of the tree; and the whole body must infallibly perish, if we remain idle spectators of the work.

John Dickinson, 1768

Although the mind is shocked at the thought of shedding human blood—more especially the blood of our countrymen—and a civil war is of all wars the most dreadful; such is the present spirit that prevails that if once they are made desparate, many, very many of our heroes will spend their lives in the cause.

Abigail Adams, 1773

We ought—and hope, will, assist one another to the utmost and bear our private sufferings with fortitude, always presenting to our minds how many generations, how many millions, depend—with regard to everything that is dear and valuable upon earth to human beings—upon our spirit and constancy at this alarming hour.

Christopher Gadsen, 1774

It is not the spirit that vapors within these walls that must stand us in stead. The exertions of this day will call forth events which will make a different spirit necessary for our salvation. Look to the end.

Who ever supposes that shouts and hosannas will terminate the trials of this day, entertains a childish fancy. We must be grossly ignorant of the importance and value of the prize for which we contend; —we must be equally ignorant of the power of those who have combined against us;—we must be blind to that malice, inveteracy and insatiable revenge which actuates our enemies in public and private, abroad and in our bosoms, to hope that we shall end this controversy without the sharpest conflicts; to flatter ourselves that popular resolves, popular harangues, popular acclamations, and popular vapor will vanquish our foes. Let us consider the issue. Let us look to the end. Let us weigh and consider before we advance to those measures which must bring on the most trying and terrible struggle this country ever saw.

Josiah Quincy, 1773

The cause is one of the utmost importance and determination of it will fix our condition as slaves or freemen.

Broadside, signed "Rusticus," 1773

To the inhabitants of the province of New Hampshire: Brethren—when we consider the unhappy condition to which you and your American brethren are reduced! when we reflect that, for near ten months past, you have been deprived of any share in your own government, and of those advantages, which flow to society from legislative assemblies; when we view the lowering clouds, charged with ministerial vengeance, fast spreading over this extensive continent, ready to burst on the heads of its inhabitants and involve the whole British empire in one common ruin—at this alarming juncture, duty to Almighty God, to our country, ourselves, and posterity, loudly demands our most strenuous exertions to avoid the impending danger. Shall we, knowing the value of freedom, and nursed in the arms of liberty, make a base and ignominious surrender of our rights, thereby consigning succeeding generations to a condition of wretchedness, from which, perhaps, all human efforts will be insufficient to extricate them? Duty to ourselves—and regard for our country, should induce us to defend our liberties, and to transmit the fair inheritance unimpaired to posterity.

> Report of a convention of 144 deputies from the towns of New Hampshire, 1775

Yesterday the greatest question was decided, which ever was debated in America, and a greater, perhaps, never was nor will be decided among men.

> John Adams (to Abigail Adams on the passage of the *Declaration of Independence*), 1776

Boston harbor a tea-pot tonight! Hurrah for Griffin's wharf!

> Popular cry, 1773

The people should never rise without doing something to be remembered—something notable and striking. This destruction of the tea is so bold, so daring, so firm, intrepid and inflexible, and it must have so important consequences, and so lasting, that I can't but consider it an epoch in history.

> John Adams, 1773

You know my opinion of the justness of our cause; you know my confidence in a righteous Providence. I seem to want nothing to keep up my spirits and to inspire me with a proper resolution to act my part well in this difficult time, but seeing you in spirits and knowing that they flow from the heart.

> James Warren (to Mercy Warren), 1775

The events of this time, may be transmitted to posterity; but the agitation of the public mind can never be fully comprehended but by those who were witnesses of it.

> David Ramsay, 1774

May the Almighty Ruler of the universe, who has raised you to independence, and given you a place among the nations of the earth, make the American Revolution an era in the history of the world, remarkable for the progressive increase in human happiness.

David Ramsay, 1783

Your taste is judicious in liking better the dreams of the future than the history of the past.

John Adams (to Thomas Jefferson), 1816

This revolution in the practice of the world may, with an honest praise, be pronounced the most triumphant epoch of its history and the most consoling presage of its happiness.

James Madison, 1792

THE CONTINUING REVOLUTION

The American War is over; but this is far from the case with the American Revolution. On the contrary, nothing but the first act of the great drama is closed.

Benjamin Rush, 1787

Can one generation bind another, and all others, in succession forever? I think not. The Creator has made the earth for the living, not the dead. Rights and powers can belong only to persons, not to things, not to mere matter unendowed with will. The dead are not even things . . . To what then are attached the rights and powers they held while in the form of men? A generation may bind itself as long as its majority continues in life; when that has disappeared, another majority is in its place, holding all the rights and powers their predecessors once held, and may change their laws and institutions to suit themselves. Nothing then is unchangeable but the inherent and inalienable rights of man!

Thomas Jefferson, 1789

The young people are right in fighting for their God-given native liberty.

Henry Muhlenberg, 1776

Every generation is equal in rights to the generation that preceded it, by the same rule that every individual is born equal in rights with his contemporary.

Tom Paine, *The Rights of Man,* 1792

The history of your own country and the late revolution are striking and recent instances of the mighty things achieved by a brave, enlightened, and hardy people, determined to be free; the very yeomanry of which, in many instances, have shown themselves superior to corruption . . . As an immediate descendant of one of those characters, may you be led to an imitation of that disinterested patriotism and that noble love of your country which will teach you to despise wealth, titles, pomp, and equipage, as mere external advantages, which cannot add to the internal excellence of your mind, or compensate for the want of integrity and virtue.

Abigail Adams (to John Quincy Adams), 1783

Remember your ancestors and your posterity.

John Dickinson, 1768

The cause of America is in a great measure the cause of all mankind. 'Tis not the concern of a day, a year, or an age; posterity are virtually involved in the contest, and will be more or less affected even to the end of time by our proceedings now.

Tom Paine, *Common Sense*, 1776

Every age and generation must be as free to act for itself, in all cases, as the ages and generation which preceded it . . . Man has no property in man; neither has any generation a property in the generations which are to follow.

Tom Paine, 1795

God forbid we should ever be twenty years without a rebellion.

Thomas Jefferson, 1787

Stain not the glory of your worthy ancestors, but like them, resolve never to part with your birthright; be wise in your deliberations, and determined in your exertions for the preservation of your liberties. Follow not the dictates of passion, but enlist yourselves under the sacred banner of reason; use every method in your power to secure your rights.

Joseph Warren, 1772

The young ascended with Mr. Jefferson to the source of those rights; the old required time for consideration before they could tread this lofty ground, which, if it had not been abandoned, at least had not been fully occupied throughout America.

Edmund Randolph, 1774

The tree of liberty must be refreshed from time to time with the blood of patriots and tyrants.

Thomas Jefferson, 1787

I own I am not a friend to a very energetic government. It is always oppressive. The late rebellion in Massachusetts has given more alarm than I think it should have done. Calculate that one rebellion in thirteen states in the course of eleven years, is but one for each state in a century and a half. No country should be so long without one.

Thomas Jefferson, 1787

Our sons, if they deserve it, will enjoy the happy fruits of their fathers' struggles.

Sam Adams, 1771

Novus Ordo Seclorum! (The New Order of the Ages Now Begins)

Motto on the Great Seal of the United States. Found on the reverse side of a dollar bill

Appendices

THE DECLARATION OF INDEPENDENCE

When in the Course of human events, it becomes necessary for one people to dissolve the political bands which have connected them with another, and to assume among the powers of the earth, the separate and equal station to which the Laws of Nature and of Nature's God entitle them, a decent respect to the opinions of mankind requires that they should declare the causes which impel them to the separation. We hold these truths to be self-evident, that all men are created equal, that they are endowed by their Creator with certain unalienable Rights, that among these are Life, Liberty and the pursuit of Happiness. That to secure these rights, Governments are instituted among Men, deriving their just powers from the consent of the governed, That whenever any Form of Government becomes destructive of these ends it is the Right of the People to alter or to abolish it, and to institute new Government, laying its foundation on such principles and organizing its powers in such form, as to them shall seem most likely to effect their Safety and Happiness. Prudence, indeed, will dictate that Governments long established should not be changed for light and transient causes; and accordingly all experience hath shewn,

This is the text of the parchment copy of the Declaration (now in the National Archives) which was signed on August 2, 1776. It is generally accepted as the most authentic of various copies.

that mankind are more disposed to suffer, while evils are sufferable, than to right themselves by abolishing the forms to which they are accustomed. But when a long train of abuses and usurpations, pursuing invariably the same Object evinces a design to reduce them under absolute Despotism, it is their right, it is their duty, to throw off such Government, and to provide new Guards for their future security. Such has been the patient sufferance of these Colonies; and such is now the necessity which constrains them to alter their former Systems of Government. The history of the present King of Great Britain is a history of repeated injuries and usurpations, all having in direct object the establishment of an absolute Tyranny over these States. To prove this, let Facts be submitted to a candid world. He has refused his Assent to Laws, the most wholesome and necessary for the public good. He has forbidden his Governors to pass Laws of immediate and pressing importance, unless suspended in their operation till his Assent should be obtained; and when so suspended, he has utterly neglected to attend to them. He has refused to pass other Laws for the accommodation of large districts of people, unless those people would relinquish the right of Representation in the Legislature, a right inestimable to them and formidable to tyrants only. He has called together legislative bodies at places unusual, uncomfortable, and distant from the depository of their public Records, for the sole purpose of fatiguing them into compliance with his measure. He has dissolved Representative Houses repeatedly, for opposing with manly firmness his invasions on the rights of the people. He has refused for a long time, after dissolutions, to cause others to be elected; whereby the Legislative powers, incapable of Annihilation, have returned to the People at large for their exercise; the State remaining in the mean time exposed to all the dangers of invasion from without, and convulsions within. He has endeavoured to prevent the population of these States; for that purpose obstructing the Laws for Naturalization of Foreigners; refusing to pass others to encourage their migrations hither, and raising the conditions of new Appropriations of Lands. He has obstructed the Administration of Justice, by refusing his Assent to Laws for establishing Judiciary powers. He has made Judges dependent on his Will alone, for the tenure of their offices, and the amount and payment of their salaries. He has erected a multitude of New Offices, and sent hither swarms of Officers to harrass our people, and eat out their substance. He has kept among us, in times of peace, standing Armies without the Consent of our legislatures. He has affected to render the Military independent of and superior to the Civil power. He has combined with others to subject us to a jurisdiction foreign to our constitution, and unacknowledged by our laws; giving his Assent to their Acts of pretended Legislation: For Quartering large bodies of armed troops among us: For protecting them, by a mock Trial, from punishment for any Murders which they should commit on the Inhabitants of these States: For cutting off our Trade with all parts of the world: For imposing Taxes on us without our Consent: For depriving us in many cases of the benefits of Trial by Jury: For transporting us beyond Seas to be tried for pretended offences: For abolishing the free System of English Laws in a neighbouring Province, establishing therein an Arbitrary government, and enlarging its Boundaries so as to render it at once an example and fit instrument for introducing the same absolute rule into these Colonies: For taking away our Charters, abolishing our most valuable Laws, and altering fundamentally the Forms of our Governments: For suspending our own Legislatures, and declaring themselves invested with power to legislate for us in all cases whatsoever. He has abdicated Government here, by declaring us out of his Protection and waging War against us. He has plundered our seas, ravaged our Coasts, burnt our towns, and destroyed the Lives of our people. He is at this time transporting large Armies of foreign Mercenaries to compleat the works of death, desolation and tyranny, already begun with circumstances of Cruelty & perfidy scarcely paralleled in the most barbarous ages, and totally unworthy the Head of a civilized nation. He has constrained our fellow Citizens taken Captive on the high Seas to bear Arms against their Country, to become the executioners of their friends and Brethren, or to fall themselves by their Hands. He has excited domestic insurrections amongst us, and has endeavoured to bring on the inhabitants of our frontiers, the merciless Indian Savages, whose known rule of warfare, is an undistinguished destruction of all ages, sexes and conditions. In every stage of these Oppressions We have Petitioned for Redress in the most humble terms: Our repeated Petitions have been answered only by repeated injury. A Prince, whose character is thus marked by every act which may define a Tyrant, is unfit to be the ruler of a free people. Nor have We been wanting in attentions to our British brethren. We have warned them from time to time of attempts by their legislature to extend an unwarrantable jurisdiction over us. We have reminded them of the circumstances of our emigration and settlement here. We have appealed to their native justice and magnanimity, and we have conjured them by the ties of our common kindred to disavow these usurpations, which, would inevitably interrupt our connections and correspondence. They too have been deaf to the voice of Justice and of consanguinity. We must, therefore, acquiesce in the necessity, which denounces our Separation, and hold them, as we hold the rest of mankind, Enemies in War, in Peace Friends.

We, therefore, the Representatives of the United States of America, in General Congress, Assembled, appealing to the Supreme Judge of the world for the rectitude of our intentions, do, in the Name, and by Authority of the good People of these Colonies solemnly publish and declare, That these United Colonies are, and of Right ought to be Free and Independent States; that they are Absolved from all Allegiance to the British Crown, and that all political connection between them and the State of Great Britain, is and ought to be totally dissolved; and that as Free and Independent States, they have full Power to levy War, conclude Peace, contract Alliances, establish Commerce, and to do all other Acts and Things which Independent States may of right do. And for the support of this Declaration, with a firm reliance on the protection of divine Providence, we mutually pledge to each other our Lives, our Fortunes and our sacred Honor.

John Hancock

Button Gwinnett	Benjamin Rush
Lyman Hall	Benja. Franklin
Geo. Walton.	John Morton
Wm. Hooper	Geo Clymer
Joseph Hewes,	Jas. Smith
John Penn	Geo. Taylor
Edward Rutledge.	James Wilson
Thos. Heyward Junr.	Geo. Ross
Thomas Lynch Junr.	Caesar Rodney
Arthur Middleton	Geo. Read
Samuel Chase	Tho M: Kean
Wm. Paca	Wm. Floyd
Thos. Stone	Phil. Livingston
Charles Carroll of	Frans. Lewis
Carrollton	Lewis Morris
George Wythe	Richd. Stockton
Richard Henry Lee	Jno Witherspoon
Th: Jefferson	Fras. Hopkinson
Benja. Harrison	John Hart
Thos. Nelson, jr.	Abra Clark
Francis Lightfoot Lee	Josiah Bartlett
Carter Braxton	Wm: Whipple
Robt. Morris	Saml. Adams
John Adams	Roger Sherman
Robt. Treat Paine	Saml. Huntington
Elbridge Gerry	Wm. Williams
Step. Hopkins	Oliver Wolcott
William Ellery	Matthew Thornton

SHORT BIOGRAPHIES

A Note on Some Terms Used in the Biographies

The men and women quoted in this book were, with a few exceptions, alive at the time of the signing of the Declaration of Independence. Many continued to live into the early years of the Republic. The years from the 1760 s to 1800 were turbulent ones. During this period there were two major views of America's place in the world. The *Tories* or *Loyalists* were conservative Americans who favored continued union with King George III and Great Britain. When the Revolution began, many of these men and women were forced to leave the country and flee to England, Nova Scotia, Canada, and other areas of the Empire. The people we call our "founders" are often referred to as "rebels," "radicals," "patriots," or "revolutionaries."

After the Revolution, Americans were again divided into two camps of political, economic and social thought. On one side were the *Federalists*, men and women who had played vital roles in the Revolution, but who felt that further radical measures aimed at economic justice and political power for the common people were unjustified and would lead to a reign of terror by the American mob. Opposing the Federalists was a group known as *Jeffersonians* (Thomas Jefferson was their leader), *Anti-Federalists*, *Republicans*, and *Democratic-Republicans*. The Republicans looked with favor on the French Revolution, and demanded sweeping economic and political reforms here at home. At times, until the election of Jefferson and his Republican allies, it looked as if the conflict between the two groups might lead to open civil war.

ABIGAIL ADAMS (1744–1818) *outspoken advocate of the rights of women, letter writer, wife of John Adams.*— Abigail Adams corresponded with many of the leading patriots of her day, and extensively with her husband while he attended the Continental Congress. In her most famous letter, she reminded her husband that it was not enough to assert that "all men are created equal," and ignore the female half of the population. She frequently denounced the lack of education for women, the absence of adulthood for women in the eyes of common law, and the denial of property rights for women.

JOHN ADAMS (1735–1826) *Second President of the United States, lawyer, signer of the Declaration of Independence, husband of Abigail Adams.*—John Adams had a long and peculiar history as a servant of his country: in 1770, he defended in court those King's troops who fired on unarmed colonists at the Boston Massacre, but by 1775 at the Continental Convention he was an ardent spokesman for immediate separation from England. As Vice President under Washington, and later as President, Adams was a leader of the Federalists.

JOHN QUINCY ADAMS (1767–1848) *Sixth President of the United States, Secretary of State, Congressman, son of John and Abigail Adams.*—Adams' presidency marked the beginning of a new era for America: the rise to power of the second generation, who followed the patriots who had fought the Revolution.

SAM ADAMS (1722–1803) *organizer, propagandist, signer of the Declaration of Independence.*—Adams was one of the most active and radical organizers and propagandists of his day. He was present at the Boston Massacre and was in Concord during the battle between the farmers and Redcoats. He gave the signal to begin the Boston Tea Party.

JAMES ALEXANDER (1691–1756) *lawyer, politician, statesman and patriot.*—Born in Scotland, he served in the forces of the Old Pretenders, during the Rebellion of 1715. Upon its defeat he fled to America and continued to speak out against the autocratic English power. During his defense of the printer Peter Zenger, who was charged with printing libel and inviting sedition in his newspaper, Alexander was charged with contempt of court and disbarred for a time.

JOHN ADAMS

ETHAN ALLEN (1738–1789) *leader of the Green Mountain Boys.*—Allen was one of the most daring military leaders of his time. His victory at Fort Ticonderoga was one of the first rebel victories. During his capture by the British he refused to desert the American cause in the face of torture and the offer of bribes.

FISHER AMES (1758–1808) *statesman, publicist, lawyer.* —Ames, a leading Federalist writer, became a major spokesman for the conservatives after the Revolution.

CRISPUS ATTUCKS (c.1724–1770)—black man who died in the Boston Massacre.

BEN AUSTIN (1752–1820) *radical organizer.*—During the Revolution, Austin wrote many patriotic essays in the Boston press. People spoke of him as second only to Sam Adams as the favorite of the Boston "mob." After the war, the Federalists considered him a terror.

BENJAMIN BACHE (1769–1798) *journalist, nephew of Ben Franklin.*—Bache was the most prominent journalist of the early Democratic-Republican Party. He founded *The Aurora.* He was once arrested on a charge of libeling the President (John Adams) and the executive.

NATHANIEL BACON (1647–1676) *colonial planter.*—In one of the earliest rebellions in the colonies, Bacon led Virginia's small farmers and lower classes against Governor Berkeley in a demand for economic justice. For a short time, Bacon's rebels seized control of the colonial capitol, but Bacon was eventually captured by Government troops and executed.

JOEL BARLOW (1754–1812) *poet and diplomat.*—Barlow, along with his friend Tom Paine, was one of the most radical thinkers of his day. After the American Revolution, Barlow went to Italy to aid in stirring rebellion in Europe.

JONATHAN BOUCHER (1737–1804) *Tory, clergyman.* —Boucher regarded the patriots' activities to resist the British oppression as seditious. When the provincial council called for a solemn fast day of protest, Boucher announced that he would preach against active resistance. He was blocked from his pulpit by a body of armed men and afterwards never preached without a pair of pistols lying on his cushion. In 1775 he fled to England.

CHARLES BROCKDEN BROWN (1771–1810) *author, patriot, women's rights advocate.*—Brown was the first person to make writing his profession in the United States. His *Alcuin* was a treatise in dialogue form on the rights of women.

CHARLES CARROLL, SR. (1737–1832) *patriot, legislator, signer of the Declaration, delegate to the Continental Congress.*—Carroll was active in the Non-Importation proceedings of 1774 and the Committees of Correspondence and Safety. He was part of a commission, with Ben Franklin and Samuel Chase, to form a union between Canada and the colonies in 1776.

BOB CENTINEL—unknown, probably an alias.

BENJAMIN CHURCH (1734–1777) *physician, poet, scholar, traitor to the Revolutionary cause.*—Church was an early and trusted member of the radical Boston Committee of Safety (other members included the Adamses and Warrens). As the Revolution began, information came to the attention of patriot leaders that led them to suspect Church of leaking secret material to the British. He was eventually tried by court martial and found guilty of "holding criminal correspondence with the enemy."

SAMUEL COOKE (1709–1820) *patriot, minister.*— Cooke was the minister of the Second Congregational Church in Cambridge. In his sermons, he often spoke of the need for a balance of powers in the government, so that neither the executive nor the legislative branch could become independent of the other.

SAMUEL COOPER (1725–1783) *patriot, clergyman.*— Cooper was not only an eloquent preacher but an active participant in the cause of liberty. The British authorities issued an order for his arrest with other leaders of the cause.

ROBERT CORAM—*political and educational theorist.*— Coram is most remembered as an educational thinker. He wrote about and opposed aggression against the American Indians.

JOSEPH COSWELL—Unknown, possibly an alias.

Sam Adams

WILLIAM CUSHING (1732–1810) *patriot, jurist.*—Before the Revolution, George III, in a move aimed at keeping a tighter rein on the administration of justice in America, proposed that American judges no longer be paid by the people of the colony they served, but rather by the British Government. As a Colonial Judge, Cushing refused to accept the King's money, arguing that the Crown was really trying to subvert justice by controlling the wages of judges. After the Revolution, he became one of the first associate justices on the Supreme Court, and administered the oath of office to Washington at his Second Inauguration.

TRISTAM DALTON (1738–1817) *patriot, Senator from Massachusetts.*—Dalton was a member of the Massachusetts House of Representatives and served as Speaker for a time.

JOHN DICKINSON (1732–1808) *propagandist, statesman, delegate to the Continental Congress.*—Dickinson became an early proponent of the rights of Americans when he anonymously authored *Letters from a Farmer in Pennsylvania* in 1765. But as events progressed, and the tone of American patriots became increasingly more radical, Dickinson found himself in the conservative branch of the movement. He served in the Continental Congress, but refused to sign the Declaration of Independence, arguing that all peaceful options had not yet been exhausted.

WILLIAM DUNLAP (1766–1839) *historian, painter, playwright.*—Dunlap believed that the theater should educate people politically. He worked for the abolition of slavery and was a staunch defender of democratic institutions.

WILLIAM EDDIS (1709–1777) *tory, Secretary to the Governor of Maryland.*—Eddis believed that the grievances of the colonists were well founded, but he argued against acts of resistance to Royal authority. When he was called before the patriots' Committee of Observation in 1776 to give "security for his behavior" or leave the colony, he chose to leave.

ANDREW ELIOT (1718–1778) *patroit, minister.*—During the occupation of Boston by the British, Eliot remained in the city and is credited with helping those who stayed behind to live under military rule.

Elbridge Gerry

King George the IIIrd

JONATHAN ELMER (1745–1817) *legislator, jurist, physician, delegate to the Continental Congress.*—Elmer published a patriotic newspaper called *Plain Dealer* and his patriotic essays were widely read. He was a supporter of Washington and Federalism.

BENJAMIN FRANKLIN (1706–1790) *inventor, publisher, ambassador, statesman, signer of the Declaration of Independence and an author of the Constitution.*— Franklin stands out as one of the geniuses of his age; a man accomplished in many fields. During the debates in the Continental Congress, Franklin's recurring message was: "We must all hang together, or we shall all hang separately." During the war, he served as America's ambassador to Europe, and was instrumental in winning France over to our side. Among his other accomplishments, he was a founder of the first anti-slavery society in the country.

PHILIP FRENEAU (1752–1832) *poet, newspaper editor.* —Following the Revolution, Freneau was an ardent and outspoken supporter of Jefferson and the Republicans. Even when threatened with jail, Freneau never let up on his newspaper attacks against the Federalist administrations of Washington and Adams. Freneau's activities led Washington to refer to him as "that rascal Freneau."

CHRISTOPHER GADSDEN (1724–1787) *radical organizer, Brigadier-General in the Continental Army, merchant.*—Gadsden was one of the leaders of the radical movement in the South before the Revolution, organizing the first Sons of Liberty in South Carolina.

THOMAS GAGE (1721–1787) *British general, Military Governor of Massachusetts.*—Gage became Governor shortly after the Boston Tea Party. His attempts to suppress the growing rebellion led him to establish martial law in Boston. He was also responsible for sending troops to Lexington and Concord in search of Sam Adams and John Hancock.

KING GEORGE III (1738–1820) *King of England.*—King George assumed the throne of England in 1760 and almost immediately encountered difficulties with his American colonies. In attempting to draw America closer to Britain, he drove the colonists to Revolution. He died a broken man, a victim of a disease that drove him insane.

Patrick Henry

Henry Lee

ELBRIDGE GERRY (1744–1814) *signer of the Declaration of Independence, lawyer, Congressman.*—Gerry was among the first patriots to call for independence in the 1770's. He was later a delegate to the Constitutional Convention, but refused to sign the document, claiming it would put America back on the track toward monarchy.

WILLIAM GODDARD (1740–1817) *journalist, printer.*— Goddard was a staunch supporter of the liberty of the press and the right of public criticism. The independent postal system that he set up was taken over by the Continental Congress and has since become the United States Post Office.

JEREMY GRIDLEY (1701–1767) *lawyer, mason, patriot leader in Massachusetts.*—Gridley was an active patriot. He was a prominent member of the militia.

ANDREW HAMILTON (c. 1676–1741) *lawyer.*—Hamilton is most noted for his defense of newspaper publisher John Peter Zenger. Though quite old at the time of the trial, Hamilton made the difficult journey from his home in Philadelphia to the courtroom in New York City to defend Zenger, and to win the first victory for freedom of the press in our history. His defense was hailed as so brilliant that he not only won the case, but was also presented with the "freedom of the city in a gold box."

JOHN HANCOCK (1737–1793) *orator, president of the Continental Congress, first signer of the Declaration of Independence, merchant.*—Hancock was considered by the British to be one of the most dangerous men of the day. He and Sam Adams were present at the Battle of Lexington on April 19, 1775, and barely escaped from Royal troops who were sent there to capture and hang them.

JOSEPH HAWLEY (1723–1788) *lawyer, patriot leader.*— Hawley is considered among the inner circle of Massachusetts patriots together with Otis, the Adamses and Warren. He wrote to Sam Adams that the people were ahead of Continental Congress in their thinking about independence.

PATRICK HENRY (1736–1799) *lawyer, orator, statesman.*—Henry was one of the most fiery speakers of his day. Long before most Americans were convinced that revolution was necessary, Henry became famous fo. uttering treasonable (i.e. anti-royal) remarks in the Virginia Legislature. During and after the Revolution, Henry served as governor of Virginia.

FRANCIS HOPKINSON (1737–1791) *statesman, musician, author, signer of the Declaration of Independence.* —Hopkinson was America's first serious composer. He designed the American flag in 1777, and served as a member of the Pennsylvania Convention which ratified the Constitution in 1787.

JOHN JAY (1745–1829) *lawyer, statesman, diplomat.*— Jay negotiated the peace with Great Britain along with Benjamin Franklin. He attended the First and Second Continental Congress and was the first Chief Justice of the Supreme Court. Jay bought slaves in order to free them. As the Governor of New York he signed the act which abolished slavery in the State.

THOMAS JEFFERSON (1743–1826) *third President, author of the Declaration of Independence, founder of the University of Virginia, leading theorist of the Revolution.*—Jefferson's concepts are as revolutionary and vital today as they were in 1776. After the conclusion of our Revolution, many Americans rallied to Jefferson and came to be known as Republicans. His electoral victory in 1800 over Adams and the Federalists was considered as much of a revolution in form as the Revolution of 1776 had been in principle.

THOMAS JONES (1731–1792) *loyalist, jurist.*—His service to the Crown up to the outbreak of war caused the patriots to be suspicious of his loyalties. He was arrested by the Continental Army and held at Fort Neck, where he wrote his observations of the war. His is the only history of the war from a loyalist's view.

SAMUEL LANGDON (1723–1797) *clergyman, President of Harvard.*—It was said of Langdon that he was elected to lead Harvard more because of his radical politics than for his accomplishments in the academic world. He was a member of the New Hampshire Convention that ratified the Constitution.

HENRY LAURENS (1724–1792) *patriot, merchant, planter, statesman.*—Laurens was elected to succeed

John Hancock as the President of the Continental Congress. He was captured by the British on his way to negotiate a treaty of commerce with the Dutch. Confined to the Tower of London he held fast to his loyalty to America. During his imprisonment he was charged for rent, and for the food and wages of his wardens as was customary at the time. He smuggled many letters out to the rebel press.

ARTHUR LEE (1740–1792) *diplomat.*—With Benjamin Franklin, Lee negotiated a treaty of aid with France. He authored *The Monitor Letters* which he said were designed to aid *The Farmers Letters* in "alarming and informing" his fellow Americans.

RICHARD HENRY LEE (1732–1794) *Senator, statesman, signer of the Declaration of Independence.*—Lee, active in his opposition to the British, led a mob to confront the Virginia stamp collectors in 1765. One year later he organized the first of the Townshend boycott actions. He, Patrick Henry and Thomas Jefferson organized the Virginia Committee of Correspondence.

DAVID LEONARD (1771–1819) *loyalist.*—Leonard was one of the leading spokesmen for the British. He published seventeen articles in defense of the British policies in America under the pseudonym of "Massachusettensis."

ALEXANDER MCDOUGALL (1731–1786) *patriot, member of the Sons of Liberty of New York, street mob leader.*—In 1769, McDougall authored a broadside entitled "To the Betrayed Inhabitants of the City and Colony of New York," which was promptly declared libelous by the British Government. He was convicted of the crime, and thus became one of the only patriot leaders to ever spend time in a British jail for his activities. Because of his popularity the Government was soon forced to let him go free.

WILLIAM MACLAY (1734–1804) *lawyer, Senator, anti-Federalist.*—Maclay first fought in the Pennsylvania militia against the British. After the Revolution, he fought in the halls of Congress against the growing powers of the executive branch of government. He was a leading proponent for economic justice, speaking out particularly against corporations, banks and other concentrations of wealth.

James Otis, early agitator against British encroachments on American liberties, spoke against the "Writs of Assistance."

JAMES MADISON (1751–1836) *Fourth President of the United States, Secretary of State under Jefferson.*— Madison authored the Declaration of Rights for Virginia, and is called the Father of the Constitution for his work on that document. He was a leader of the Republicans, and opposed the establishment of U.S. banks.

GEORGE MASON (1725–1792) *statesman, planter.*— During the Revolution, Mason remained in Virginia where he fought for progressive advances within the State. Later, he was a leader of the movement to include a bill of rights within the new Constitution.

JONATHAN MAYHEW (1720–1766) *clergyman, patriot.* —Mayhew's discourse "For Resistance to Unjust Authority" in 1750 was called the opening gun of the Revolution by John Adams. From the pulpit he defended popular disobedience to commands that were contrary to God's. After the repeal of the Stamp Act his sermons counselled the people to observe the laws but to be watchful for their rights.

GOUVERNEUR MORRIS (1752–1816) *statesman, diplomat.*—Morris was a conservative until the Battle of Lexington. Being a member of the aristocracy he feared the social upheaval that he thought would follow a "democratic" revolution, but he did hold fast to the American cause. He favored a strong, centralized government.

HENRY MUHLENBERG (1711–1787) *Lutheran minister.* —Muhlenberg created a network of German Lutherans in the middle colonies.

JAMES OTIS (1725–1783) *propagandist, agitator.*—Otis was one of the earliest public enemies of King George and his policies. He began his radical agitating in the early 1760's and was an anti-government force during his days in the Massachusetts legislature. In 1769, he was beaten by an angered British official, and never recovered his senses fully. Otis, a firebrand of the Revolution, died the year the war ended, struck by a bolt of lightning.

JOHN PAGE (1743–1808) *patriot and legislator.*—Page was Lieutenant Governor under Patrick Henry, an influential member of the colonial legislature, and a member of the convention that drafted the Virginia Constitution.

TOM PAINE (1737–1809) *revolutionary propagandist, inventor, international radical organizer.*—Paine sparked the Revolution with his pamphlet, *Common Sense*. During the darkest days at Valley Forge, Paine began a series of articles entitled *The Crisis* that rallied the Continental Army. After the Revolution, Paine went to England and France where he played important roles in radical democratic movements.

PHILLIPS PAYSON (1736–1801) *patriot, minister, scholar.*—Payson was minister at the Congregational Church in Chelsea, Massachusetts. Among his most famous sermons are "Sermon on the Battle of Lexington" and "Death of Washington."

LORD HUGH PERCY (1742–1817) *British military officer.*—Percy led the relief column at Lexington and Concord that saved the British forces from being wiped out by the Minutemen. He was opposed to the policy of the British Government in America, and eventually resigned his commission.

SIMON PETER—unknown, probably an alias.

JOSIAH QUINCY (1744–1775) *lawyer, propagandist.*—Quincy, one of the youngest patriot leaders, was also one of the most radical. He wrote extremely effective pamphlets on the dangers of a standing army, and denounced merchants who broke the patriots' boycott of British goods. Returning from a mission to Europe, he died on the boat without witnessing the revolution he had worked for.

DAVID RAMSAY (1749–1815) *historian, physician.*—Ramsay wrote a comprehensive history of the Revolutionary war. He was a close friend of Benjamin Rush and a delegate to the Continental Congress.

EDMUND JENINGS RANDOLPH (1753–1813) *member of the Continental Congress, aide-de-camp to General Washington.*—Randolph defended Aaron Burr on a charge of treason in 1807. He refused to sign the Constitution with George Mason because he thought it was insufficiently democratic.

BENJAMIN RUSH (1745–1813) *physician, patriot, member of the Continental Congress.*—Rush was one of the founders of the first American anti-slavery society.

He established the first free dispensary clinic in America. He was one of the signers of the Declaration of Independence and treasurer of the U.S. Mint. He has been called the father of American medicine.

GRANVILLE SHARP (1735–1813) *English Whig and humanitarian.*—Sharp was a leader in the anti-slavery movement in England, and a friend of the American cause during the Revolution.

JOHN TAYLOR (1753–1824) *agriculturist, political writer.*—Taylor was important to the passage of the Twelfth Amendment. He called the Hamilton banking measures "usurpations upon Constitutional principles aimed at the creation of an aristocratic paper junto and the subversion of democratic government."

ISAIAH THOMAS (1749–1831) *editor, printer.*—Thomas was the editor of *The Massachusetts Spy* which was one of the leading patriotic newspapers of the time. He was a Minute Man at Lexington and Concord. He published *Mother Goose's Melody* and *Fanny Hill.* After the Revolution he was one of the leaders of tax resistance movements.

CHARLES THOMSON (1730–1824) *former indentured servant, patriot.*—Thomson, although a non-delegate was the Secretary to the Continental Congress from 1774–1789. He was chosen by the Indians to keep their records of the proceedings at the Treaty of Easton in 1757 because of his reputation of fairness and integrity. He was a leader of the left wing of the Sons of Liberty and John Adams called him the Sam Adams of Philadelphia.

JOHN TRUMBULL (1750–1831) *poet, artist, playwright.*—During the Revolution, Trumbull contributed a running series of satirical comments on British policy and administration to local newspapers in New Haven and Boston. He was one of the principal portrait artists of the age.

JOHN TUCKER (1719–1792) *minister.*—Tucker was pastor of the First Parish Congregational Church of Newburyport, Massachusetts.

CHARLES TURNER (1732–1815) *patriot, writer and orator.*—Turner was minister at the town of Duxbury, Massachusetts.

JAMES WARREN (1726–1808) *legislator, patriot, husband of Mercy Otis Warren.*—Warren was one of the leading patriots of Boston. When the Massachusetts legislature removed itself from Boston and the control of Gage to a rural town, Warren was appointed President.

JOSEPH WARREN (1741–1775) *physician, orator, patriot.*—Warren was one of the most respected orators of his day. He was killed at the battle of Bunker Hill. A monument stands where he fell and commemorates him and the patriotism of his countrymen.

MERCY OTIS WARREN (1728–1814) *poet, historian, letterwriter.*—Mercy Warren wrote the most complete, and radical, history of the Revolution. After the Revolution, she sided with the Republicans, even though John and Abigail Adams—both Federalists—were her best friends.

GEORGE WASHINGTON (1732–1799) *First President of the United States, Commander of the Continental Army.* —Washington was the most popular and powerful figure of his day, so popular in fact, that as the war neared an end, some of his officers offered to make him king and military dictator of America. Washington was appalled at the idea, and strongly rebuked the men who had made the suggestion.

NOAH WEBSTER (1758–1843) *teacher, compiler of the first American dictionary.*—Webster conceived of the new dictionary as a revolutionary act of getting rid of everything British. He believed that the most important thing taught in schools should be history and the most important thing taught in history should be the Revolution.

SAMUEL WEST (1730–1807) *minister, author.*—West's sermons dealt harshly with the tyranny of England. He served as a chaplain during the Revolutionary War and deciphered the treasonable note from Church. He was one of the members of the committee appointed to frame the Constitution for Massachusetts.

WILLIAM WHIPPLE (1730–1785) *patriot.*—Whipple was an influential member of the New Hampshire Popular Party.

STEPHEN WHITE (1718–1794)—Minister in Windham, Connecticut.

PETER WHITNEY (1744–1816) patriot, minister at the Congregational Church in Quincy, Massachusetts.

JOHN WISE (1652–1725) *patriot, minister.*—Wise was one of the most radical and influential New England preachers before the Revolution. At one point, he was tried and found guilty of opposing the Royal Government's attempt to impose a new tax on Massachusetts. After his conviction, he wrote a pamphlet that was reprinted by the patriots of Boston and used as an argument for greater freedom in America.

JOHN WITHERSPOON (1723–1794) *minister, patriot.*—Witherspoon came to America to be the President of the College of New Jersey which later became Princeton. He is the only clergyman that signed the Declaration of Independence.

JOHN WOOLMAN (1720–1772) *minister.*—Woolman was a Quaker leader and advocate for the abolition of slavery. He opposed conscription and taxation for military supplies.

GOVERNOR WILLIAM WRIGHT—Royal Governor of Georgia arrested by the patriots in 1775 and confined to a rebel prison during the war.

A SYLLABUS AND STUDY GUIDE TO THE AMERICAN REVOLUTION

EIGHT BOOKS FOR A SHORT SEMINAR

The Spirit of '76, Carl Becker, A. M. Kelly, 1966.

The Spirit of '76, Henry Steele Commager and Richard B. Morris, Harper and Row, 1967.

The American Revolution Considered as a Social Movement, J. Franklin Jameson, Princeton University Press, 1926.

Private Yankee Doodle; being a narrative of some of the adventures, dangers, and sufferings of a revolutionary soldier, Joseph Plumb Martin, Ed. by George F. Scheer, Little Brown, 1962.

The Origins of the American Revolution, John C. Miller, Stanford University Press, 1957.

The Birth of the Republic, Edmund Morgan, University of Chicago Press, 1956.

The Stamp Act Crisis, Edmund Morgan and Helen Morgan, Collier Books, 1963.

Sources and Documents Illustrating the American Revolution, Samuel Eliot Morison, ed., Oxford University Press, 1965.

BOOKS FOR YOUNG READERS

Women in Eighteenth-Century America, Mary S. Benson, Kennikat Press, 1966.

John Adams and the American Revolution, Catherine Drinker Bowen, Little, Brown, 1950.

Look to the Mountain, Le Grand Cannon, H. Holt, 1942.

The Spirit of '76, Henry Steele Commager and Richard B. Morris, Harper and Row, 1967.

Drums Along the Mohawk, Walter Edmonds, Little, Brown, 1937.

Paul Revere and the World He Lived In, Esther Forbes, Houghton Mifflin, 1942.

Johnny Tremaine, Esther Forbes, Houghton Mifflin, 1945.

The Adventures of Christopher Hawkins, Christopher Hawkins, New York Times, 1968.

Private Yankee Doodle; being a narrative of some of the adventures, dangers, and sufferings of a Revolutionary soldier, Joseph Plumb Martin, George F. Scheer, ed., Little, Brown, 1962.

Rag, Tag and Bobtail; The Story of the Continental Army, Lynn Montross, Barnes and Noble, 1967.

The Negro in the American Revolution, Benjamin Quarles, University of North Carolina Press, 1961.

Colonists in Bondage; White Servitude and Convict Labor in America, Abbot Smith, University of North Carolina Press, 1947.

The American Revolution, George Otto Trevelyan, D. McKay, 1964.

The Secret History of the American Revolution, Carl Van Doren, A. M. Kelly, 1973.

The Great Rehearsal; the Story of the Making and Ratifying of the Constitution, Carl Van Doren, Viking Press, 1948.

Mutiny in January, Carl Van Doren, A. M. Kelly, 1973.

Sally Wister's Journal, Sarah Wister, New York Times, 1969.

THE COLONIAL BACKGROUND OF THE AMERICAN REVOLUTION

Errand into the Wilderness, Perry Miller, Belknap Press, 1956.

The Puritans, Perry Miller, Doubleday, 1956.

The Intellectual Life of Colonial New England, Samuel Eliot Morison, New York University Press, 1956.

Colonists in Bondage; White Servitude and Convict Labor in America, Abbot Smith, University of North Carolina Press, 1947.

Gentleman Freeholders; Political Practices in Washington's Virginia, Charles S. Sydnor, University of North Carolina Press, 1952.

The Peaceable Kingdom; New England Towns in the Eighteenth-Century, Michael Zuckerman, Knopf, 1970.

The Colonial Era, Herbert Aptheker, International Publishers, 1966.

THE BRITISH BACKGROUND

British Opinion and the American Revolution, Dora Mae Clark, Yale University Press, 1930.

Preliminaries of the American Revolution as Seen in the English Press, Fred J. Hinkhouse, Octagon Books, 1969.

A History of England in the Eighteenth-Century, William Lecky, A.M.S. Press, 1968.

The Origins of the American Revolution, John C. Miller, Stanford University Press, 1957.

DEVELOPING THE REVOLUTIONARY MOVEMENT

The Coming of the Revolution, Lawrence Gipson, Harpers', 1954.

From Resistance to Revolution, Pauline Maier, Knopf, 1972.

Founding of a Nation, Merrill Jensen, Oxford University Press, 1968.

The History of the American Revolution, David Ramsay, Russell and Russell, 1968.

Toward Lexington, John Sly, Princeton University, 1965.

The Eve of the Revolution, Carl Becker, Yale University Press, 1921.

The Boston Tea Party, Benjamin Labaree, Oxford University Press, 1964.

The Stamp Act Crisis, Edmund Morgan and Helen Morgan, Collier Books, 1963.

Seedtime of the Republic, Clinton Rossiter, Harcourt, Brace, 1953.

The Boston Massacre, Hiller Zobel, Norton, 1970.

OUR FOUNDING RADICALS: THEIR PHILOSOPHY AND STRATEGY

Ideological Origins of the American Revolution, Bernard Bailyn, Belknap Press, 1967.

Pamphlets of the American Revolution, Bernard Bailyn, Belknap Press, 1965.

The Lamp of Experience, Trevor Colburn, University of North Carolina Press, 1965.

The American Revolution: A Constitutional Interpretation, Charles McIlwain, Macmillan, 1923.

Sam Adams, John C. Miller, Belknap Press, 1936.

Chronicles of the American Revolution, Hezekiah Niles, University Press, 1965.

Tracts of the American Revolution, Merrill Jensen, Bobbs-Merrill, 1967.

The Declaration of Independence, Carl Becker, P. Smith, 1933.

Common Sense and Other Political Writings, Tom Paine, Bobbs-Merrill, 1953.

THE AMERICAN TORY

Democratic Republican Societies, Eugene Link, Columbia University Press, 1942.

The American Tory, William H. Nelson, Oxford University Press, 1961.

Origin and Progress of the American Rebellion, Peter Oliver, Stanford University Press, 1961.

The Loyalists in the American Revolution, C. H. Van Tyne, P. Smith, 1929.

THE AMERICAN REVOLUTION AND THE MILITARY

The American Rebellion, Sir Henry Clinton, Yale University Press, 1954.

George Washington in the American Revolution, James Flexner, Little, Brown, 1968.

The Campaign of 1781 in the Carolinas, Henry Lee, Quadrangle Books, 1962.

Rag, Tag and Bobtail; The Story of the Continental Army, Lynn Montross, Barnes and Noble, 1967.

The History of the Origin, Progress and Termination of the American War, Charles Stedman, New York Times, 1969.

The American Revolution, George Otto Trevelyan, D. McKay Co., 1964.

The Voices of '76, Richard B. Wheeler, Thomas, Y. Crowell, 1972.

Battles of the American Revolution, Henry Beebe Carrington, New York Times, 1968.

THE AMERICAN REVOLUTION AND LABOR

The American Revolution, Herbert Aptheker, International Publishers, 1960.

The Sons of Liberty in New York, H. B. Dawson, Arno Press, 1969.

Laboring and Dependent Classes in America, Marcus Jernegan, Ungar, 1960.

Government and Labor in Early America, Richard B. Morris, Harpers' Torchbook, 1965.

The Colonial Merchants and the American Revolution, Arthur Schlesinger, Columbia University Press, 1918.

THE BLACK CONTRIBUTION TO THE AMERICAN REVOLUTION

The Negro in the American Revolution, Herbert Aptheker, International Publishers, 1940.

The Negro in Colonial New England, L. J. Greene, Kennikat Press, 1966.

The Negro in the American Revolution, Benjamin Quarles, University of North Carolina Press, 1961.

The Black Presence in the Era of the American Revolution, Sidney Kaplan and the Smithsonian Institution, New York Graphic Society Ltd., 1973.

WOMEN AND THE AMERICAN REVOLUTION

Women's Life and Work in the Southern Colonies, Julia Cherry Spruill, Norton, 1972.

Colonial Dames and Good Wives, Alice Morse Earle, Ungar, 1962.

Customs and Fashions in Old New England, Alice Morse Earle, Corner House Publishers, 1969.

Familiar Letters of John Adams and Abigail Adams during the American Revolution, Charles Francis Adams, ed., Books for Libraries Press, 1970.

Correspondence Between John Adams and Mercy Warren, C. F. Adams, ed., Arno Press, 1972.

Sally Wister's Journal, Sarah Wister, New York Times, 1969.

History of Women's Suffrage, Susan B. Anthony, Elizabeth Cady Stanton, Matilda Jocelyn Gage, and Ida Harper, eds., 1881.

Century of Struggle: The Women's Rights Movement in the Revolution, Eleanor Flexner, Belknap Press, 1912.

THE AMERICAN REVOLUTION AND THE AMERICAN INDIAN

History of the American Indians, James Adair, Johnson Reprint Corp., 1968.

The Indian and the White Man, Wilcomb Washburn, New York University Press, 1964.

The Iroquois in the American Revolution, Barbara Graymont, Syracuse University Press, 1972.

DIPLOMACY AND THE AMERICAN REVOLUTION

The Diplomacy of the American Revolution, Samuel Bemis, Appleton-Century, 1935.

English Whiggism and the American Revolution, George

H. Guttridge, University of California Press, 1942.
The Peacemakers, Richard B. Morris, Harper and Row, 1965.
John Adams, Vol. II, Page Smith, Doubleday, 1962.

DEBATE: WAS THE AMERICAN REVOLUTION A DEMOCRATIC REVOLUTION?

The American Revolution Considered as a Social Movement, J. Franklin Jameson, Princeton University Press, 1926.
The American Revolution: Two Centuries of Interpretation, Edmund Morgan, ed., Prentice-Hall, 1965.
Causes and Consequences of the American Revolution, Esmond Wright, ed., Quadrangle Books, 1966.

**PEOPLES
BICENTENNIAL
COMMISSION**

1346 Connecticut Avenue, NW
Washington, DC 20036
(202) 833-9121

You Can Join With The New Patriots!

The PBC is involved in a massive campaign to revive the democratic principles and ideals that sparked the American Revolution.

Our commission is made up of citizens like yourself who are dedicated to making this country live up to its revolutionary promise. We would like you to take part in the peoples campaign for the Bicentennial by joining the PBC Committee of Correspondence. Membership in the Committee of Correspondence is $10.00. You will receive a year's subscription to *Common Sense* magazine and the following materials: "Community Programs for a Peoples Bicentennial;" "Student and Teacher Programs for a Peoples Bicentennial;" "Religious Participation in the Bicentennial;" and a special youth activity guide for the Bicentennial. All four guides contain scores of program ideas, activities, suggestions, as well as historical material about the Revolution and its implications for today. Also included in the kit are study guides, an American history magazine, and posters and buttons. Enclose a check or money order for $10.00 payable to the Peoples Bicentennial Commission, Washington, D.C. 20036.

We have produced a complete Bicentennial display package of books on the American Revolution: "In the Minds and Hearts of the People." The display, especially suited to library and school use, contains eight large posters based on quotes from the founding fathers and mothers, thirty reproductions of Revolutionary era engravings, captions and headlines describing the major events and the themes of the American Revolution, and a Syllabus and Study Guide compiled by Dr. Page Smith, PBC senior staff historian and a Bancroft Award-winning author. "In the Minds and Hearts of the People" can be ordered for $20.00 from the Peoples Bicentennial Commission, Washington, D.C. 20036.

All these materials are for organizing and participating in local Peoples Bicentennial efforts.

The Bicentennial materials can help you spread the message of '76 in your community.

Peoples Bicentennial Commission
Programs and Activities

• PBC has developed educational materials and social action programs during the Bicentennial for organizations ranging from the National Council of Churches and Campfire Girls to the Child Care Council of America.

Thousands of libraries, churches, fraternal clubs, schools, civil associations, etc., are curently using materials and programs specially developed by the PBC.

• Affiliated PBCs are now operating in twenty-eight states. They are engaged in a wide range of public educational programs and social action campaigns.

Thousands of citizens in all fifty states are paid members of the PBC Committee of Correspondence and are actively engaged in their own organizations and communities around PBC programs.

• The PBC radio series, *The Voices of '76*, is being aired on a daily basis by 935 radio stations across the U.S.

• The PBC television series, *The Voices of '76*, is being aired on an ongoing basis by 102 TV stations in major metropolitan areas throughout the country.

• The PBC feature service is sent to over fourteen thousand general and specialized media publications and journals.

Hear ye! Hear ye!

Celebrate America's 200th Birthday with special programs prepared by the

PEOPLES BICENTENNIAL COMMISSION

SPEAKERS AVAILABLE THROUGH THE

BANTAM LECTURE BUREAU

For information, contact

BANTAM LECTURE BUREAU, Dept. BLB-19,
666 Fifth Avenue, New York, N.Y. 10019

_____Send me FREE complete BLB brochure with listings of more than 50 lectures.

My organization plans_____programs each year.

NAME_____

COLLEGE/ASSOCIATION_____

ADDRESS_____

CITY_____STATE/ZIP_____

TELEPHONE_____

BLB-19— 1/75

If you need information in a big hurry, just call us. (212) 765-9650.